Values for Our Time

AN ESSAY INTO
THE WONDER AND WOE
OF THE WORLD

Woody Wood

Devolve!
LEICESTER, ENGLAND

Published by *Devolve!*
13 Biddulph Street
Leicester
England
LE2 1BH

Other acknowledgments in text and reference pages

Values for Our Time / Wood —1st ed.
ISBN 978-0-9931126-0-7

Cover design and typography by The Artful Bookman
Printed and bound by imprintDigital.com

To all those colleagues
who have inspired stages of the journey

Abstract

The essay opens with a brief look at knowing that questions its purposes, distinguishes levels of understanding and challenges the subjective-objective opposition.

The remainder of the essay unfolds in three chapters or Stories.

The Natural World Story attempts to list the patterns and features of our universe in a narrative that is more integrative than conventional science yet more grounded than metaphysics. In the process it introduces some concepts considered relevant to the following stories, including the two aspects of the Universe and the derivation of morality from its 'mechanics'.

Additional notions introduced include the two thresholds, modes of being and creative belief.

The Social Story begins by arguing that social animals like humans actually live on the interface between collectivity and autonomy and that the consequent tensions inform all social issues.

It goes on to explore social modes, social structure and social types. The fundamental and complementary relation between divergent (leaderful) and convergent (followful) types is pivotal to the Story.

The notions of immanence and transcendence lead on to the beginnings of a critique of the Enlightenment, while identity and identification introduce the more general topic of meme transfer.

Introduction of the tool of social mapping, or space geography, allows examination of the interplay of authority, alienation and co-operation and draws attention to the Jacobin and Neoliberal grand narratives that civil society must both challenge and reach accommodations with.

The final sections of the Story consider sexuality as a social factor before taking note of some deeper issues and closing with a list of core concepts.

The Ecology and Values Story puts the population issue centre stage in arguing the conflict of purposes – and hence values – between the needs/wants of humanity and the diverse needs of our biosphere. In this context it confirms the notion of values warrior as one who has made that choice in favour of the planet, of Gaia.

Arguing, as have others, that the sixth extinction is now well under way, it looks to what can and should be done both to reduce human impact on the biosphere and to ensure that the values of immanence, emotional intelligence and sharing are well represented among the survivors.

In noting the scale of the necessary values reversal, the obstacle of the values of liberal morality is brought into focus and the strengths and weaknesses of Nietzsche as a values pathfinder are considered.

In view of the daunting tasks facing those who choose to identify as values warriors, the notion of values struggle is more carefully defined, distinguishing its use in a social context from its meaning in ecology.

In the last section of this Story alternative courses of action are considered in turn, including their probability/possibility, their values implications and their effect on the values mix of survivors.

The short end note is a personal acknowledgement of responsibility.

Introduction

We may have a problem. With climate changing, human population escalating, resources dwindling, pollution spreading, species dying … we may have a problem.

To face up to any problem one usually needs to understand in order to act. Maybe the place to start is to understand understanding – knowing.

Why know? The answer seems so obvious that a more challenging question is: why not know? It can be better not to know, for some people some of the time: to avoid pain or for fear of closing down the future. For all of us not knowing can preserve mystery in our world and a precious innocence. Then there is Nietzsche's powerful challenge to the insatiable thirst for knowledge of Enlightenment science[1] :

"He does not love the things he knows, but has spirit and appetite for an enjoyment of the chase and intrigues of knowledge – up to the highest and remotest stars of knowledge! ... It is the last knowledge that seduces him. Perhaps it too proves a disillusionment, like all knowledge. And then he would have to stand to all eternity transfixed to disillusionment and himself become a stone guest, with a longing for a supper of knowledge that he will never get; the whole universe has not a single morsel left to give to this hungry man."

Given the often compelling reasons for knowing, to know or not to know becomes a matter of judgement. One mark of the sage (see below) is the wisdom to make this judgement.

Before proceeding, a side note and apology. Words matter. "You cannot stand outside language." Labels are not just descriptions/pictures but tools. (Wittgenstein re-crafted his whole philosophy when he realised this.[2]) As with all tools, words may be right for the job in hand or not, sharp or not. If this essay fails its intention, if it fails to mobilise the new warriors for the new values, the failure is of the words to communicate the concepts, the situation, the task.

Taking a closer look at the urge to understand, we can note two very different approaches.

The first is passionate, often immediate, unashamedly prejudiced to outcomes, situation driven by some combination of internal drives/needs and external threats/opportunities: "That predator will take me/that prey will escape if I/we don't think/act fast"; "How do I play it with this potential mate?"; "The house is on fire … grab an extinguisher? … get out fast?"; "My friend is sad, distressed: how do I respond?" and so on.

We can call this Dionysian[3] understanding. Its strengths are rapid calculation (calling on experience) for rapid response, plus intuitive empathy, recognised today as emotional intelligence. Often it was all our ancestors needed. Its weakness becomes obvious with the larger scale more complex problems facing us today (including problems that may call ourselves as actors into question). Dionysian understanding always seeks the most direct answers. It is intuitively reluctant to seek broader, more interlocked, longer range models for understanding and possible action. [Braziers School of Integrative Social Research[4] was founded partly to address this 'resistive' attitude: what follows is relevant to its themes.]

The second approach is dispassionate, 'neutral', 'objective', nominally curiosity driven "knowledge for its own sake". More realistically power driven: mastery of the universe through knowledge. (In fact much investigation today is funding driven but that's another story.) "Why does the apple fall to the ground?"; "How far away are the stars?"; "What drives evolution?"; "What happens if I drop this acid into this rabbit's eye?"…

Let us call this Apollonian[5] understanding. Its strength lies in seeking for a breadth and depth of knowledge that Dionysian understanding lacks. Its greatest fruits have been seen in the technologies that have transformed our world: from military technology (who can doubt that a nuclear warhead is vastly superior to a spear?) to the medical and sanitation technologies that have given many of us cleaner, safer, longer lives … and fed the human population explosion.

The weaknesses of Apollonian understanding are two. First, its claim of disinterested investigation is an abdication of moral responsibility (both for what it pursues and for what it omits to pursue). [To his credit, Albert Einstein[6] is reported to have said (when the first atom bomb was exploded): "I wish I had been a watchmaker."] Second, its assumption that the scientific observer stands outside the field of study, supposedly detached from the world, makes the method more problematical when the focus turns to critical questions in human social affairs. As Henri and Henriette Frankfort[7] put it in 'Before Philosophy': "Man does not quite succeed in becoming a scientific object to himself."

So far this sketch of what we have called Apollonian and Dionysian understanding has crudely lumped together the scientist, the philosopher, the sage and the poet: all with a view on 'the big picture'. (Of course the same human being may know themselves, or be recognised by others, as more than one of these.) We need to finesse this a bit, at least with some sub-headings for further exploration.

Scientist (classical)

Assumptions: Objective Reality; Detachment of Observer

Focus: Usually Narrow

Aim: Extend Boundaries of the Understood

Method: Testable Hypotheses

Core Tool: Measurement

Philosopher (mainstream)

Assumptions: Logical Universe; Knowability

Focus: may be Narrow or Broad

Aims: Clarity or Comprehension

Methods: Introspection; Logical Manipulation

Core Tool: Thinking

Sage (non-theistic)

Assumption: Interconnectedness

Focus: Broad

Aim: Wisdom

Methods: Absorption of Internal and External Experience; Holistic Integration

Core Tools: Thinking; Intuition; Apprehension

Poet (deep)

Assumption: Suffering Universe

Focus: Broad

Aims: Communication; Re-presentation

Methods: Absorption of Value Loaded Experience; Re-transmission with Emotional Impact

Core Tools: Intuition; Apprehension; Empathy; Medium of Expression

As already stated, these categories refer to modes of being, which particular persons may fit well or badly. A notable example is Nietzsche: not a very good philosopher, in terms of the logic test. A 'hardcore' philosopher such as Wittgenstein would consider most of his statements to be meaningless. So clearly the seriousness with which he is taken today (even by those keen to refute his outlook) is recognition of his status as a sage (on the above criteria) and it is argued that this is how we should regard him.

As a further aside: homage to the Dark Mountain project. Here we search for wisdom through consideration and thought swapping: the wisdom of the poets is deeper still.

Now given the scale and complexity of the issues that we face going into the middle of the twenty first century, the widely (but not universally) agreed urgency of some of them, the sobering possibility that we are part of the problem ... there is a case for transcending both Dionysian and Apollonian understanding with an approach that draws on the strengths of both. As with the Apollonian, going as broad and deep as may be needed to grasp our situation. As with the Dionysian, unashamedly knowing that we are passionate participants in what we observe, willing outcomes according to our values – even as those values are open to challenge by the integrity of our pursuit of understanding.

Since we have dispensed with the myth of disinterested knowledge, it would not be unreasonable to call this synthesis Motivated understanding. Whatever, this will be the basis of the rest of this exploration.

A footnote on objectivity. It should already be clear that the terms 'objective' and 'subjective' are not helpful. For the description of our reality more grounded concepts will be introduced below. From the point of view of the knower, integrity is the core notion. It was always so. In the forenoon of empirical science it was not, as they believed, their objectivity that rightly distinguished those earnest investigators from the astrologers, the transmuters, the charlatans, the quacks ... but their integrity. (Some of the foremost scientists have understood integrity as the anchoring notion[8].)

For the rest of this essay there will be an attempt to explore what we know, think we know or are edging towards knowing – in three stories or chapters: -

The Natural World Story.

The Social Story.

The Ecology and Values Story.

CHAPTER 1

The Natural World Story

The intention of this Story is to example an integrative approach across all aspects of existence.

If the universe is taken to be universal *by definition* – to include everything – then by this definition it includes *everything*. There is no beyond. There are no levers.

The universe has **patterns** and **features**. Without them it would be impossible to describe it or act in it. These are recognisable rather than provable, as with the axioms of geometry. If we distinguish, as far as possible, its patterns or properties – its *scaffolding* – from its features, its *content*, then some of them may be noted as below:

Key Patterns of the Universe

First Pattern

The properties or patterns of the universe are **universal,** so far as we know. One way of stating this is "nature does not know metaphor or simile". For example, the shops competing (and sometimes complementing) in the High Street are not just like the plants competing (and sometimes complementing) in the hedgerow: the same pattern is on display, despite the very different 'chemistry'. For another example, the distortion of space-time geometry in the presence of an intense gravitational field is not just like the distortion of perceived social reality in the presence of intense sexual urges: they are both aspects of an underlying pattern that becomes visible in various contexts.

Second Pattern

The universe is **nodal.** There are certain nodes, relationships, orbits, vibrations, spaces etc that are 'permitted', stable, resonant. This means that it is not 'anything goes'. It does not fill at once and everywhere every possibility of being and not being. (A total everything would be nothing – rather like a sheet of paper totally blackened by written information.)

Third Pattern

The universe is **probabilistic.** This means that it does its thing with fuzzy interactions, fuzzy logic, fuzzy energy and fuzzy everything else. However, since there is always a *main* probability for any element or interaction the universe is *approximately* logical and definite. For example, Newton's patterns (let's not say laws) remain approximately true – and useful – in a relativistic space-time universe. This is helpful to human and other brains that have evolved logic as a tool for mapping it and thinking about it. It is even more helpful in that the chair you are about to sit on will *probably* be there...

Against this, the minor probability of a paradoxical outcome always exists, especially at the limits of scale – e.g. sub-atomic physics – and at high levels of complexity – e.g. how can war be *both* glorious and obscene?

Because of this paradoxical element the foundation stone of the rational approach to the world, the first axiom of all logical reasoning: 'A' cannot *both* be 'B' and 'Not B' ... does not strictly hold for our universe.

Fourth Pattern

The interactions of the universe are **reciprocal.** There are no one-way effects. For example, a walnut exercises a gravitational pull on the sun, albeit a tiny one. One of the shock discoveries of quantum physics was that the observer/measurer could not be independent of the entity being measured. The act of measurement affects the reality (for instance location) of the object, just as the information (rays) from the revealed object affects the measuring device employed. This principle of reciprocity is now accepted by mainstream science – with one glaring exception: considered under the sixth pattern below.

Fifth Pattern

The universe **self-creates.** By definition (see above) there can be no external creative forces acting on a dumb universe, bringing it to life. Rather, the universe is smart, dynamic. (It is likely that coming to apprehend and empathise with its purposes will form a critical part of the new wisdom.) It is a moot point whether this smart dynamic could be 'explained' in terms of myriad feedback loops.

To a more limited extent this fifth pattern applies also to its parts. They are not just passive entities responding to the ground rules set for them and the forces acting on them, but potentially creators and self-creators. We too are "both creators and clay" (Nietzsche[9]).

Sixth Pattern

The universe experiences itself, suffers and wills, just as we do – as all its parts must do. Yet it still remains something to be observed and measured, theorised about, by scientists and others. Thus it can be said that the universe has an 'inside' experiencing aspect and an 'outside' observable aspect. The shorthand terms **inside** and **outside** will be used to describe these two aspects of our reality.

The first philosopher-sage to recognise this was Schopenhauer[10] – except that his emphasis (for the inside) was on the active, *willing* aspect, to the neglect of its/our passive, *suffering* aspect. Hence his title: 'The World as Will and Idea'. None-the-less this was the first formal statement of that which the poets have long known: that 'the world' is not just on the other end of a telescope or microscope. Rather we experience it at first hand, can have empathy with it, for we are part of it.

After Schopenhauer came Nietzsche: "what does deep midnight's voice contend?"[11] Sigmund Freud[12] – out of fashion today and arguably not a very good therapist – will one day be recognised as the first *scientist* of the inside of the Universe. He acknowledged his debt to Nietzsche.

This connectedness between the inside and the outside of the universe cannot be exempt from the Fourth Pattern: reciprocity. In our own human experience, just as matter affects mind (e.g. through stimulants etc) so mind must affect matter, even though the effects may be minute in 'normal' circumstances.

Mainstream science tries to respond to this challenge by reducing the experiencing inside of the universe to an 'epiphenomenon' and relegating investigations of possible effects to 'paranormal' status, not a proper subject for scientific investigation – despite substantial funding for military research in this area. At least the behavioural psychologists[13] of the twentieth century were consistent in denying the very existence of the inside of the universe – including their own minds! [This subject is explored further in the Social Story.]

It is clear from the above that these two aspects of a *single* reality require different tools of apprehension. Thus the labels inside and outside are to be preferred to 'subjective' (which today carries the implication of inferior, prejudiced 'unscientific' knowing) and 'objective' (which implies detached, neutral, 'scientific' knowing of an Apollonian reality).

Lastly, as the most complex thing, the universe experiences itself with more complexity, more completeness than any of its parts: just as our experience of ourselves is more complex, more 'alive' than (say) the self-experience of a stone, which 'only' experiences its tensions and atomic vibrations (or so we think).

Seventh Pattern

This property emerges out of observation of the features (content) of the universe but appears to be so critical and context transferable that it is listed here as a pattern. It can be expressed in the form: -

"Every ***means*** strives to become an ***end***."

It may bear some relation to Newton's first pattern of dynamics: that bodies set in motion have a momentum in their own right.

There are many examples. According to Richard Dawkins[14] the very first carbon chain molecules may have been add ons, tools, for early silicon based life, *means* to its existence. If so, they soon became *ends* in themselves: the ubiquitous life forms of today. Closer to home, money was created as a *means* of exchange. Today it is fair to say that money (not man) is the measure of all things. It has become a self-replicating *end* in its own right. In the words of Norman.O.Brown[15] "Capital breeds". Another example is the political party. Often founded in pursuit of certain social ideas, a *means* to them, it sooner or later becomes an *end* in its own right, committed to its own preservation and the pursuit of power. Other examples could be given, you can probably think of some.

Some Features of the Universe

First Feature

Our whole dynamic universe comprises an interaction, an interplay, between **form** and **intropy***. You could say that they are locked in endless combat: form seeks to contain, to freeze intropy while intropy aims to liberate, to destroy form. Yet also in vital partnership: form without intropy would be a dead, frozen Universe (despite the energy locked into form); intropy without form would be a blinding flash of annihilation. [*Intropy can be defined as useful, dynamic, form changing energy. It is significant that nineteenth century science uses entropy – the uselessness of energy – as its measure. The possibility of intropy generation is denied by this same science.]

This tension-loaded partnership of opposites is reflected at all levels. In human affairs the male tends to be attracted to the *form* of the female and the female to the *energy* of the male.

Second Feature

The universe has **structure.** Structure may be defined as distinctive form in which the *relationships* between 'things' (simple form) become greater 'things', cascading upwards to ever-greater levels of complexity. Another way of putting this is that 'things' are bundles of relationships between lesser 'things', which are...

Thus the relationship or interaction between two (or more) 'things' can be thought of as a **creative interface**, an important concept in understanding our world. The forming and dissolving of such relationships can be seen as acts of *creation* and *un-creation*. The obvious examples are in physics/chemistry/biology, where atoms interact to form molecules; simple molecules complex into giant organic molecules, and so on. In each case the distinctive structure defines the properties of the greater whole. The miracle of the *creative interface* literally creating the new can be observed in many situations.

Third Feature

Beyond structure, the universe often displays **dynamic structure - process.** This can be defined as intropy acting in form or intropy driven form. These active systems may not amount to self-maintaining or self-replicating life but they are a pre-requirement for it. 'The Web of Life' by Fritjof Capra[16] gives a good description of this powerful feature of our world.

Fourth Feature

Equally amazing is that matching dynamic structures can **resonate** with each other, even when they are not in physical contact. Tuning forks are the classic example. Resonance shows up everywhere, literally a universal feature. It can be thought of as intropy transfer, as in the electrical transformer. Also as information transfer or communication: in telephony, in computers, in human memory and association. Also as emotional linking: allowing empathy and social intelligence: *caring* as central to bonding in social groups.

Fifth Feature

When a dynamic structure is in a state of *tension* (e.g. a stretched spring) it will act, if it is able, to come to a position in which it is no longer in tension. This can be thought of as the 'normal' position or *norm*. Thus any structure with tension has **norm seeking** properties. An engineer would say that it possessed potential energy, potentially form changing energy – in our language intropy. The general proposition is that "a system in tension always seeks to relieve itself". This is true across the board, from mechanical to organic to living systems; from stretched springs to human sexual tension.

Sixth Feature

When a dynamic structure is able to *actively maintain itself*, making use of the intropy flowing through it and being consumed by it, then there is the essence of **life**. In practice such systems are organic and one of their tensions is for the food that provides the driving intropy (and the spare parts).

Seventh Feature

So far the norm seeking behaviour of dynamic structures (including living systems) has been described in mechanical terms. However, the sixth basic property of the universe reminds us that all structures have an internal *experiencing* side as well as an external side that can be described by an observer.

From the inside norms are experienced as *goals* and the drive towards them, the goal seeking, as **purpose** or **will**. No wonder *will* was such a central concept for both Schopenhauer and Nietzsche.

Eighth Feature

The existence of purpose (will) in living systems has significant implications, especially when the experiencing is recognisably conscious in our terms.

First, purpose implies *identity*: the 'I' that has the purpose. [More on identity later.] Second, purpose implies *suffering*: experiencing the hunger etc (and also the satisfaction of tension release). Third, purpose implies *an environment*: (benign, neutral or hostile) in which the structure/creature must act. Fourth, purpose implies *resistance* (whether passive or active): work to be done. Fifth, purpose implies *means*: the method or strategy that is used to achieve the purpose. Sixth, purpose implies the possibility of a *conflict* of wills – and a whole new feature...

Ninth Feature

Purpose conflict implies *morality*. Thus in a few short concept steps we have proceeded from the basic 'mechanics' of the universe to *morality*: one of the central concepts of this essay. One can distinguish ethics, a complex subject in sophisticated social groups, from *morality*, defined in the following way: *"when two purposes (wills) conflict each is a threat to the other, immoral from the standpoint of the other, even when they are not recognised as such and even when they are embodied in the same system/creature."* On this definition moral conflict is a widespread feature of dynamic systems such as living (including social) organisms, not confined to social contract situations. Guilt can be a by-product of internal purpose conflicts. To sum up: morality is just a coded word for purpose: "that is morally wrong" means "you offend my/our/His purpose".

Continuing the Natural World Story

'Facts' and Descriptions

Before noting more 'facts' about the structure and content of the natural world, there is a case for separating – as far as possible – these 'facts' from the words and labels used to describe them. This is often called the **category** and **content** problem.

How long is that pencil? The answer will depend on whether the ruler you bring to it is in inches or centimetres (or whether you measure it against your hand). Now consider shoe making and wearing. To a good chiropodist there is no such thing as a size seven foot (male or female!) because every foot is unique: the *categories* break down at this level of scrutiny. However, to a shoes manufacturer needing to make thousands, to the retailer and to the shopper in a hurry (not able to afford handmade shoes), the notion of a size seven shoe is useful. There may be a case for half sizes in shoes, and/or for A, B, C, D etc width fittings. Here we come across the important concept of the **trade off**, in this case between accuracy and simplicity. [This question of category and content will become relevant in the Social Story, when we consider social types.]

The Two Thresholds

Aristotle[17] had the concept of the *golden mean*, both in nature and as a guide to human action. Intuitively feels about right but as a conceptual tool you can't do a lot with it. Ivan Illich[18] – radical thinker of the twentieth century – advanced this to the notion of the **two thresholds**, which has very wide application in describing the natural world, as well as for social and ecological understanding.

Used in conjunction with the concept of a *trade-off* between competing needs or goals, it implies a workable region or **comfort zone** between two limiting thresholds, crossing which can signify failure or disaster in different ways. Take the case of spiders, in which the digestive tract passes through the brain. This has been described as a Catch 22 between "inability to swallow food and inability to have the intelligence to catch it". Since spiders do thrive, adapted as blood sucking creatures, there is obviously a *comfort zone* between the two thresholds that would threaten survival.

In the more general case of the relation between a species or group and its environment there is a *lower threshold* below which the species or population loses the struggle with nature and fails to survive. Since it is reckoned that over 95% of all species that have existed are now extinct, this is the line most often crossed.

However, a species may also be so effective that it is in danger of crossing the *second threshold* and devouring its environment. [Plate 1]

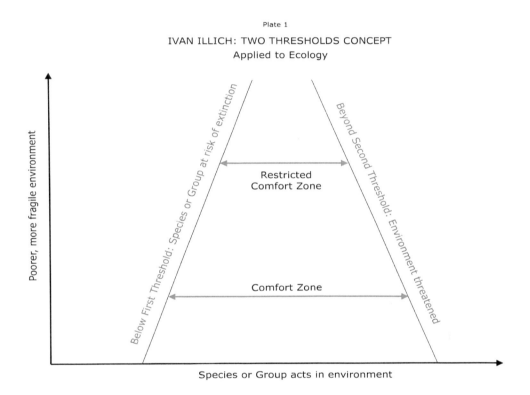

Plate 1

IVAN ILLICH: TWO THRESHOLDS CONCEPT
Applied to Ecology

This has actually happened to some groups in island environments and has been averted for others by a drastic change of strategy. Most species and populations exist in some sort of balance with their environment – in the *comfort zone* between the two thresholds.

A comfort zone is never assured. A change in the environment – say an ice age – may drastically narrow the comfort zone between the two thresholds.

Apart from its application in the natural world, the notion of the two thresholds is a helpful tool in looking at social affairs and in addressing some values problems. These aspects will be examined in the following stories.

In the field of critical thinking with a view to action, the limiting *threshold*s to the 'health zone' of *provisional* knowing are total doubt (inability to act) and total certainty (inability to doubt). Aiming for the 'effective action zone' between these two dysfunctions was one of the founding objectives of Braziers School of Integrative Social Research[4], considered in the context of social types in the Social Story below.

Ivan Illich had important things to say on many aspects of society including schooling, work and leisure. He remains a largely neglected source of insight into our woes. Parts of the following explorations are indirectly influenced by his wisdom.

Reprise on the Creative Interface

Again and again it is on the interface or interaction face between two (or more) relatively stable structures or systems that new levels of complexity, new leaps of creativity, can be noted. For example the chemical interface between 'P' doped and 'N' doped silicon creates the dynamic region (in the silicon chip) that allows signal amplification and switching, information manipulation and transmission to take place: giving rise to the whole information technology revolution that is sweeping our social world.

Bohemian quarters in cities, with their artistic creativity and challenge to social norms, have frequently arisen on the interface between run down inner city areas and more affluent 'middle class' districts. Again, it is on the interface between two (usually jealously guarded) academic disciplines that new leaps in understanding can take place. The confused birth of social psychology from the disciplines of sociology and psychology is very relevant to the Social Story.

More generally, the birth of 'original thought', of new insights, frequently arises from placing two known concepts alongside each other: putting two and two together, you might say. In the Social Story we will explore a significant creative interface between autonomy and collectivity. The point worth noting here is that creative interfaces are not without their tensions and difficulties.

Fulfilment

It is obvious to anyone who has lived a little that *fulfilment* is not the same thing as pleasure. A person may experience considerable fulfilment in caring for a loved relative or friend who is seriously ill – even though some of the tasks will hardly be pleasurable. Conversely someone who is existentially un-fulfilled may take pleasure in tastes and sensations. Indeed, over-indulgence (e.g. an alcohol habit) may be compensation for lack of fulfilment. All of us take pleasure in gratifying needs of course, while knowing that this is transitory. The joy of an ice cream (say) cannot be extended by eating a hundred ice creams.

Taking the view from the universe observed as a 'thing', we have already noted that systems in tension act (if possible) to relieve that tension and that this corresponds (on the experiencing side) to the gratification of hunger (for example) by taking and eating food.

Now one of the noted patterns of Newtonian dynamics is usually stated: "work is done when a force moves its point of application". The amount of work done depends on the resistance that the force has to overcome. If there is hardly any resistance then the work done is trivial. On the other hand, if the resistance is too great for the force (as when trying to push a car with the brakes on) then no work is done.

The corresponding statement on the inner (experiencing) side of the universe may be put as: "fulfilment is achieved when a purposive activity drives towards a goal". Again the amount of fulfilment depends on the resistance that the purpose overcomes. If the resistance is too great to permit progress then we experience frustration. If there is hardly any resistance then the exercise is trivial: as our ancestors knew well, there is far more fulfilment in catching/growing and preparing food than in getting it 'on a plate'.

Since new needs and obligations to act are constantly arising, the concept of a *cycle of fulfilment* emerges. This is consistent with the cycles of life, the cycle of the seasons and the cyclic view of time that all peoples once had. With the Enlightenment has come the concept of linear time and linear progress towards some point at the end of the rainbow. Taken together with many other aspects of the modern world (more on this later) one can see why, even for those of us who do not experience the perpetual frustration of continuous hunger, so many people today are un-fulfilled, in their work and in their lives.

Against this background the revolutionary achieves fulfilment in the struggle – though may also be prone to idealising 'the revolution' at the end of the rainbow.

Stability of Form

It has already been noted that form, complex structured form, is a key feature of our universe. Form may be very stable (like ancient rocks); subject to gradual decay (like us) or very unstable (like a snowman on a warm day). Now an important special case is **meta-stable** form. Apparently stable and solid, or at least ongoing, it can be 'kicked' into a different arrangement or **mode** by some impact or event.

In engineering and other disciplines much use is made of the principle of meta-stable form in mechanical and other devices where the response to a series of identical inputs is required to produce non-identical outputs, because the device has been nudged into a new *mode* – counters are a simple example.

For dynamic, active, interacting form (like, say, you) this new mode of being can result in different behaviour. On the corresponding inside of the universe this change of mode may be experienced as a change of **mood**. If you are angry or upset your response to something I say or do may be completely different to what it might have been (and what I might have expected!) in your previous mode/mood.

Meta-stable behaviour is common in more complex structures (such as social groups) and is a significant element in the Social Story to follow.

Beyond Apollonian Science

Among the Patterns of our universe, the Fourth Pattern – reciprocal interactions – and the Sixth Pattern: the inside and outside aspects of all things, have already been noted. Taken together, these patterns imply a special case of the *creative interface*: not between two entities but in this instance between two *aspects* of a single reality. It has been argued that since 'matter' can obviously affect 'mind' then 'mind' must have the potential to affect 'matter' to some degree, however minute these effects may be in 'normal' circumstances.

In recent years there have been major advances in neuroscience, exploring the *correlation* between neural pathways etc and mental states. Impressive as these additions to our knowledge certainly are, they remain exercises in Apollonian understanding: knowing a world of facts and objects.

Julian Jaynes in 'The Origin of Consciousness in the Breakdown of the Bicameral Mind'[19] seeks to demonstrate a previous human ability, gradually lost to us, of directly apprehending something of the wisdom of the universe, of 'communicating with the gods' – or rather (in Jaynes' view) of believing that you are doing so – in what we might now call an altered state of consciousness. Although the book may be criticised on several levels (for instance it requires a very special interpretation of human self-consciousness to argue that it was so late in developing) it remains a tour de force as a journey through ten thousand years of human social evolution.

The relevance is that Hammurabi and Moses could still talk directly with their gods in certain circumstances. Half a millennium later this was no longer possible. The Assyrian altar carving, reproduced by Jaynes and copied here, of the tyrant king Tukulti-Ninurta I approaching and then kneeling before the *empty* throne of his god is surely one of the most potent images from any culture. [Plate 2]

Plate 2   BREAKDOWN OF THE BICAMERAL MIND

Tikulti-Ninurta I approaches the <u>empty</u> throne of his god Nuska – c 1250 BCE

In ancient Greece the rise of the rational/sceptical approach that was to give birth to modern science – re-discovered in the Renaissance and consummated in the Enlightenment – can be said to have brought down the curtain on this direct apprehension. Yet it was in this same Greece that one of the last channels of communication was kept open for a thousand years through the Delphic Oracle. Jaynes records that the most effective instruments of the Oracle were young uneducated country girls.

For all 'left brain' activities, all scepticism, worldliness, cynicism render impossible any empathy, any resonance, between our own suffering, willing selves and our suffering, willing universe. A message to scientists everywhere: stop measuring! …at least on Thursdays…

Towards an Integrative Science

Even for those who wouldn't accept the previous conclusion, there has been growing disquiet (including among scientists) at the limitations of mainstream science with its deterministic, reductionist approach. A developing understanding of non-linear systems, with their unpredictable outcomes, has contributed to this unease.

As far back as the 1940s Lancelot L Whyte[20], a radical scientist, was arguing for a 'new' science that was: (i) integrative across all wisdom, rather than subject and category bound; (ii) about dynamic processes rather than 'facts'; (iii) socially and morally embedded rather than values neutral. Some of the thinkers who have taken up this challenge are referred to in this essay.

Belief and Faith

But can belief create? At the very least we are obliged to be open minded on this, and pay attention to those who argue that it can. If the universal pattern of reciprocity *does* hold across the interface, then the story of Tinker Bell in Peter Pan has it exactly right. The implications for a new science and an old/new wisdom are wide ranging. Future peoples, if they exist, will honour the achievements of Apollonian understanding yet recognise its narrowness of focus, its self-chosen limitation to one half of the universe. One of many possible 'applications' is faith enhanced intropy generation as both a driver of social economic activity (as oil is today) and a regenerator – rewinding the universe.

Do the gods exist? Assuming that intropy driven life has reached sufficient levels of complexity on numbers of planets across endless galaxies as to make the *need* for gods – as explanations, as bearings to life, as moral guides, as mentors to peoples and (sadly) as instruments of social control, manipulation and oppression – a potent force, then countless gods obviously *will* exist in the minds of all those who believe in them, need them.

This thesis tentatively goes further. If belief **is** a creative force in our universe, then there is a sense in which these myriad gods have reality as internal interconnections, as influencers, in proportion to the number of followers who have faith in them. Should this be the case then the task for those concerned about the malevolent effects of religious belief (Karl Marx: "religion is the opium of the people"[21]) is not to dismiss such beliefs as fantasies but to work at reducing the need, to offer positive alternative understandings, bearings, guides to action.

Perhaps this process is under way on our particular planet in a partial shift from religion with a capital "R" to spirituality (often with a small "s"). Thus it is possible to honour and serve Gaia, conceived as the spirit of our living planet [see Ecology and Values Story], Galaxia (term proposed by Isaac Asimov[22]) or even the spirit of our dynamic and suffering universe (could be called … you know).

Lastly, a quote from Friedrich Nietzsche. Not the (in)famous "God is dead" line put into the mouth of a madman (actually a comment on the loss of bearings in the society he saw around him). This one is a judgment on all totalitarian, absolute standpoints[23]:

> "The gods are dead. They died laughing when an old wrath beard of a god said:
>
> 'Thou shalt have no other gods but me' "

CHAPTER 2

The Social Story

It is often stated that humans are social animals and in one sense this is obviously true. Yet in another sense it is only half true.

If we take **collectivity** and **autonomy** as opposing concepts, then at one extreme the hive bees and the cells of our bodies are fully collective: they have no choice, no prospect of even partial autonomy. (Note that being in physical contact or not is not the defining characteristic.) At the other end of the spectrum the bumble bee and the amoeba have the joys and perils of high levels of autonomy.

In comparison 'higher' animals like apes exist on the *creative interface* between *collectivity* and *autonomy* – and experience the tensions of both. This is particularly true of humans who are 'programmed not to be programmed'. For many humans, especially today in our crowded cities, autonomy remains an ideal even when interdependence is the reality. Our existence – living with the tensions of this creative interface – has implications for the Social Story. Note that Robert Ardrey[24] in 'The Social Contract' makes essentially the same point using his own key concepts of *order* and *disorder* for collectivity and autonomy. These tensions run through all political debate: between those who see the importance of our autonomy and those who put emphasis on mutual support; on the team.

Social Modes

Just as individual organisms can be 'flipped' into different modes of behaviour and self-experience, so too can group organisms, including human groups.

Marx and Engels[25] had argued that 'primitive communism' was the natural mode of archaic human communities such as the agricultural village. However in 'Energy and Economic Myths', a wide ranging collection of essays on social economics, Nicholas Georgescu-Roegen[26] argues that, under normal conditions, **fair play** between partially autonomous and self-reliant families was the dominant mode and guiding morality. This would include some collective activities such as bringing in the harvest. An example of the *fair play* principle would be that if one family had, as its first field strip, a very fertile and productive patch then its second strip might be on less good soil than other families. How well the strips were worked was down to the efforts of the family concerned. This trade-off between autonomy and collectivity could be stable over time.

Now it is well known that when any group is under threat (or perceives itself to be so) there tends to be a closing of ranks with both social and psychological consequences. (Various studies have shown that in times of war rates of mental illness and suicide fall as individuals focus less on themselves and more on the group – see identification discussion below.) For our purposes this shift may be seen as a flip from the normal **fair play** mode to a **war communism** mode. Something very similar happens in the individual animal (patterns of the universe are universal, remember) with a flip from the parasympathetic nervous system: business as usual; blood priority to the digestive and other organs ... to the sympathetic nervous system: action stations; blood priority to the muscles and brain.

The flip into *war communism* mode can happen in both small and large social groups. Certainly in England and the other home countries this was dramatic in the Second World War. There were still spivs and chancers out for number one of course (spiv became a term of total contempt) but the overall spirit was of solidarity and stoicism. In a bye-election held in Chelmsford in early 1945 a Common Wealth[27] candidate took this Conservative seat on a platform of the abolition of private property!

Now the lag effect (in our bodies too) means that the war communism mode/mood persists for a time after the danger has passed. In the 1945 General Election two communists were returned, leading some to believe that this was a trend. In fact war communism was fading and a *fair play* mode of 'autonomy plus caring' (e.g. the National Health Service was widely popular) was returning. [No space here to discuss class issues.]

The balance at the interface between autonomy and collectivity is a delicate one and other group modes are possible. Large-scale modern societies, with their emphasis on *aspiration* for the individual, mask our mutual interdependence for basic survival. The illusion of high levels of autonomy (especially if you have at least some money) makes possible a flip (or rather slide) from fair play mode into an individualist or **alienation** mode. This process has become very evident in modern 'free' consumption driven societies where the 'slave producers' are mostly out of sight. A much older flip was into the shamed/wronged, 'get you back' or **feuding** mode, exampled by the Trojan War and still prevalent among mafias and drugs gangs. Lastly, when the pressures on any group or society are simply too great there can be a flip into **anarcho-panic** mode, with self-survival instincts to the fore amid social breakdown. This may yet be the fate of large, complex modern societies.

The Size Question

Which leads into *size* as a significant (and usually overlooked) component in the structure and dynamics of human societies. [Honourable exceptions are Leopold Kohr[28] and his disciple E.F. Schumacher[29]. Their thinking puts the implications of size centre stage.] Here only one aspect of this major social factor will be noted – linking stability of form [see Natural World Story above] with the social modes just discussed.

Both historical and contemporary studies of 'traditional' societies show that under conditions of low population density the fair play mode may be *stable* over many generations. Likewise the historical and sociological record shows that in larger human groups/societies with what one might term medium population density the fair play mode may best be regarded as *meta-stable* – may be flipped (e.g. by social disturbance) into another, more stressful mode.

Finally, in high population density mass societies – as in the age of the zero geography, hyper-communicated 'global village' – the traditional fair play mode through which human society evolved becomes observably *unstable*. Social campaigners and would-be social engineers may wring their hands at this – yet miss the critical link to population density that makes it inevitable. [The vital questions of population and population density are discussed in the Ecology and Values Story below.]

Social Structure – Social Types

Since all organisms have **structure**, usually a complex structure of interacting parts or elements, it is inconceivable that human social groups could be an exception.

Yet there is a silent consensus to downplay and even deny social structure in both popular and academic sub-cultures. It is argued that this is partly because "man has never succeeded in becoming a proper object of study to himself" and partly because the dominant ideology of individualism and aspiration strongly resists both classifying/labelling people as social types and conceding reality/identity to human groups over and above the individuals who comprise them. In the literature one can find twenty-five centuries of examination and discussion of psychological types (for we are fascinated with ourselves as individuals) and yet very little about the broader social types that give structure to human (and animal) groups.

To start with some definitions. **Social types** are essentially structural complements and components for the functioning of the whole group (but with some dysfunctional variations). **Psychological types** are essentially neurotic imbalances/departures from some nominal ideal human being (but with productive consequences; e.g. the autistic element in mathematical aptitude).

Two ideas networks that have attempted to explore the nature of social types (and sub-types) are firstly the Braziers School of Integrative Social Research[30] aiming to develop, among other strands, the early twentieth century work of Wilfred Trotter[31]; and secondly the *Devolve!* network[32] (with a devolution standpoint and drawing on coal face experience of the 1970s communities movement). Interestingly both sources suggest a 5% - 95% primary ratio in basic human social types. The Braziers exploration has (since 1950) been more focussed on differences within the 5% 'differentiated' (their terminology) primary type, working with the **'sensitive'** and **'resistive'** sub-types identified by Trotter, leading to the methodology of *sensory* and *executive* modes of being and deciding. The *Devolve!* network continues to seek to understand the primary relationship between **Convergent** and **Divergent** types. (Their terminology: terms adapted from their use in educational psychology.)

Devolve! has argued that the **complementary** interplay between *Convergent* and *Divergent* social types is fundamental to understanding social structure and process in social group creatures. This remains true even in the human case where the high flexibility of responses to context makes the notion of rigid types problematical when examined 'close up' at the level of a few individuals: here it may be more appropriate to speak of someone being in *Convergent mode* in a given situation – say for example normally convergent at work yet often leaderful in the family or in their social activities. However, when 'standing back' to consider larger social groupings such qualifications are 'averaged out' and the basic social types – *Convergent* and *Divergent* – become useful tools of description.

In Convergent – Divergent theory the distinction is **not** one of intelligence, ability or class upbringing (though any of these may play a secondary role in enhancing/inhibiting the confidence levels that seem to be a contributory factor in type formation). Rather the distinction between these basic human (and animal) *complementary* types lies in responses to *power* and *responsibility*: strictly **powerlessness** and **responsibility**. In essence the Divergent, leaderful, type will in most situations seek to avoid powerlessness even where this means accepting the 'pain' of responsibility. In contrast the Convergent, followful, type will usually avoid responsibility and accept powerlessness in the sense of conceding social decision making to others.

Derivation of Types

The emergence of these observable types in biological and social evolution from early primitive forms is a matter for speculation/investigation. One possible line of argument starts by noting that creatures, from the simple amoeba onwards, tend to move *towards* 'pleasure' and *away* from 'pain'. A problem then arises when both drives are in play, when both exist in tension, when a *choice* has to be made. To take a hypothetical example, a parched gazelle (say) comes to the edge of a water hole on the African savannah and scents the presence of leopard or other predator nearby. The choice is between the 'courageous' option of making a dash for water and the lower (immediate) risk 'un-brave' option of backing away.

Now in terms of organic life *power* may be defined as the ability to act to secure pleasure/satisfaction (or conversely *powerlessness* as the inability to so act). Likewise *responsibility* may be defined as willingness to risk potential pain. Since "every means strives to become an end" (seventh pattern of the universe) then (potential) pleasure seeking can become sublimated into powerlessness avoidance and pain avoidance may likewise be sublimated into responsibility avoidance.

[The notation 'powerlessness' is preferred because of the ambiguity in the notion 'will to power' between will to power in the sense of ability to act, to tackle life, which is critical to all living creatures and 'will to power over' or 'will to dominate' which certainly exists but is not universal. This ambiguity exists in the thinking of Schopenhauer, Nietzsche, Adler[33] and Robert Ardrey[34], among others.]

It is argued that in complex creatures this sublimation *has* taken place and that in social creatures a new possibility opens up when faced with 'the hard choice'. Most members of the group no longer need to go for the high-risk 'brave' strategy because "someone else will do it". The way is open for the emergence of complementary types – with advantages for both and for the group as a whole. Hence Convergence and Divergence as defined above.

Complementary Types

It is important not to value-judge these basic types as superior v inferior. *The complementary relation is a fundamental category in its own right* – alongside equal and unequal relations.

This complementary partnership is necessary to the structure and functioning of the social group, much as yeast and dough need each other in leavened bread. In fact the majority Convergent type has some very positive qualities, including a capacity for team working and an existential ability to 'be'.

In contrast the minority Divergent type *can* display a neurotic drive (to infinity?) plus both instinctive and ego rivalries that range all the way from the fight to the death among newly emerging queen bees to the power struggles of mafias and empires. In traditional small groups this trait can be said to perform a survival function in providing clear leadership. In modern large-scale, loosely bonded societies and into our troubled future it becomes one of our greatest unsolved problems. [See Ecology and Values Story]

A further assumption to be avoided is that the Divergent type (say) automatically corresponds to the Alphas in social hierarchies and pecking orders. (The chapter on the Alpha Fish in Robert Ardrey's 'The Social Contract'[34] is recommended for a lucid explanation of social relations in animals from this perspective.) While there is often an overlap in practice and Divergents are naturally leaderful when called upon, the criteria are different: in one case to avoid powerlessness in forced choice situations – in the other some combination of the drive to dominate and the need for bearings, for a role. There will be examples around you of the unassuming divergent: you might even be one.

One partial response to conflict between Divergents as social group numbers have increased has been the emergence of different **arenas** in which one Divergent or more might dominate, compete or even collaborate. In the earliest hunting groups one dominant Divergent would lead, often out of respect for prowess and wisdom, with younger hopefuls waiting in the wings. As awe for nature crystallised into nature spirits and the need to placate them, the role of shaman – claiming such powers – became distinct from the role of chief. Thus there were now two complementary *arenas* in which Divergents could be leaderful.

When the Convergence – Divergence dimensions are set against (say) Morton Deutsch[35] social relations 'types', Ivan Illich's two thresholds concept and/or the social memes spectrum of Spiral Dynamics[36] ... a whole new range of questions and clues regarding social structure comes into view. Here is a discipline in the making. [Plates 3, 4 plus Plate 6]

Plate 3

Social Types with Values Dimension

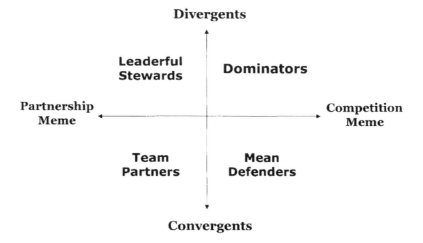

Plate 4

COMBINING MORTON DEUTSCH WITH IVAN ILLICH

(On the equality/inequality dimension only in this case)

	MORE EQUAL RELATIONS		
CO-OPERATIVE ETHIC	Reciprocal Partnership between Equals	Head to Head between Equals	COMPETITIVE ETHIC
	Complementary (Convergent – Divergent) Role Based Partnerships	Hierarchies and Pecking Orders	
	Nurturing Partnership	Dominance and Subjection	
	MORE UNEQUAL RELATIONS		

N.B. The Illich spectrum (between limiting thresholds) may also be applied to the Co-operation – Competition axis, with interesting results. Real relations have aspects of both.

Social Types in Mass Society

There is more to say on Convergents and Divergents in mass societies, especially those nominally democratic. To continue a previous theme the number of *arenas* for Divergents has multiplied. Peer group rivalries within, say, an academic discipline will exist on a different wavelength to those in, for instance, a civil service department. Unfortunately the poker players at the top table are still capable of damaging societies and sending nations to war – and the theory should be able to explain why.

The defining characteristic of Divergence is the avoidance of powerlessness – being willing to shoulder responsibility (including social responsibility) in expectation of helping to shape the social environment and the policies of the social whole. Divergents thus defined – social divergents – are the true yeast of the social mix. Some of the best local councillors (for example) fall into this category. If the 5% figure is anywhere near the mark this would suggest two and a half million potential leaderful stewards in England alone: the bedrock of a true, **_organic democracy_**.

However, there are a certain number of Divergents with an ego drive for power that takes a social/political form. Let us call these ego Divergents or aspirant Divergents. (One feature of individualist-alienated society is that _aspiration_ to wealth or power becomes a core value.) A small proportion of these sub-types, by a combination of luck, ability and ruthlessness, manage to climb the greasy pole to a point where they have the potential to cause significant damage, either de-stabilising the social fabric or prosecuting wars or both. In the 1980s Margaret Thatcher was an iconic example. [Plate 5]

Plate 5

DOMINATORS AND DOMINATED IN MASS SOCIETIES

On to Convergents. Without in any way denigrating the positive qualities of Convergents as team players ready for complementary, sometimes followful, roles and capable of living in the moment (immanence) ... there are certain characteristics that become problematical (or worse) in large-scale societies. Apart from the primary objective of avoiding responsibility, "not sticking your head above the parapet" there are a number of tactical advantages to Convergence.

The first of these is proxy power: identifying with strong leaders, basking in the reflected glory of their victories. The second is the right to free moans, especially when things are going less well. Some argue that moaning is endemic in England ('whingeing poms' as the Aussies would have it) possibly a consequence of nearly one thousand years of our subjection and denigration since the occupation. A third advantage to Convergence is the ability to switch sides between competing Divergents and then enjoy the spectacle of the mighty falling. Many of the 'ordinary people' who were cheering Maggie when 'our boys' were re-taking the Malvinas were also cheering in inner city streets when she was toppled.

From here it is not hard to see that the result of combining one person one vote democracy (regardless of responsibility level) with a powerful, unelected and Convergent influencing media has been an ***unholy alliance*** between clique(s) of ego Divergents and a sufficient majority of naturally followful Convergents to keep most concerned Divergents – natural responsibility takers – permanently out of power: condemned to the side-lines. In autocratic societies with ruthless yet charismatic leaders the *unholy alliance* is likely to be even more unshakeable – unless and until the Convergents 'flip'.

There is no real answer to this dilemma within mass society (assuming that organic democracy – power to the responsible – is not achievable from this starting point). Only when political ecology leads again to human scaled human groups will healthy Convergent – Divergent partnerships become options. Appropriate size is a pre-condition for social Divergents to play their part in a caring and integrated social fabric.

Immanence and Transcendence

In dynamic physical systems in tension, whether a stretched spring or a hungry human, there is normally an end purpose or goal that can be reached, in principle, in the real world. And on the inside of the universe these activities can lead on to experiencing fulfilment and the cycles of fulfilment, as already discussed. Engineers give the responses to tensions that achieve these positive results the unfortunate name of negative feedback. However, when the responses actually increase the tension and excitement then the norm or goal is off the chart, off the map; it is notional, it does not exist in the real world. Engineers call this process positive feedback. In physical systems the wildly increasing tension, the ever-rising graph, reaches a break point at the limits of that actual system. A classic example is the terrible howl in a public hall (say) when the microphone is placed too near the speakers. Nature makes use of this essentially unstable dynamic in a few rare cases such as sexual orgasm, where the increasing tension leads to a break point and (in the male) to ejaculation.

In the mental world of imagination it is different. There are no limits; there is no break point. Anything can be imagined. Wonderful nirvanas can be imagined, even to the detriment of action and fulfilment in this our real world. Perhaps it started with dreams of deceased relatives, alive in happier times. Certainly the notion of a better world, more real and lasting than this 'world of appearances', became easy to peddle, easy to transmit as a meme or belief system (see below), amid the misery of the first mass slave societies. For slave and master alike these *transcendental* nirvanas offered the prospect of cheating death.

One might have thought that with the birth of the Enlightenment and the Age of Reason the meme of the *transcendental* goal would cease to find fertile soil. In fact the threats to ***immanence***, to valuing and living in the now, were multiplied. Not only was traditional faith in unworldly worlds largely undimmed, not only did most empirical scientists have no difficulty in keeping their faith and their science in separate compartments but a new *transcendentalism* was born out of the Enlightenment concepts of linear time and infinite progress. It was now possible to envisage new vistas of perfection, new nirvanas in our physical world but postponed into a distant future that degraded the present. Since these notions of progress towards abundance and perfection have little regard for physical restraints (resources for instance) they also threaten the future of living things [see Ecology and Values Story]. Lastly, they make it harder for Divergents to recover a valid leaderful role in social groups in harmony with both our environment and our immanent reality.

Identity and Identification

Apart from their physical existence and structure, dynamic systems – including living organisms like people and social groups – can be said to carry (or embody) programmes that determine their behaviour, both in responding to stimuli and in seeking to release their intropy. On the inside of the universe these are experienced as urges, needs, fears and values. Among human beings and their cultures, 'programmed not to be programmed', these behaviours and self-experiences can be almost infinitely flexible and 'detached' from obvious physical advantage. The concept of transmittable ***memes*** as the carriers of different perceptions and behaviours was put forward by Richard Dawkins[37] in 'The Selfish Gene' and developed by Susan Blackmore[38] and others.

The parallel with genes has been criticised (as a transmittable replicator a meme has more in common with a virus than a gene). With this caution, the meme can be a useful tool for understanding the spread of new values and attitudes among social groups. The issue of memes generally in the social story will be returned to later. For the moment our focus is on the meme of self-perception, of *identity*. This can meet the need for bearings, for self-worth, and its particular form can be influenced by social role and valuations reflected from others. Robert Ardrey lists *identity* as a crucial animal need, even ahead of the need for 'stimulation' (his term for fulfilment and intropy release through activity) and the need for security.

Every organism identifies with itself as a coherent whole as it experiences itself (whether 'consciously' or not). What happens when a group of organisms comes together to create (permanently or otherwise) a more complex coherent whole (whether a multi-celled creature or a flock of birds)? Is the new identity of the whole located in this or that cell/bird? Clearly not: it is diffused throughout the creature/flock. The parts have identified with the whole, while still being 'aware' of themselves and their condition (e.g. healthy/unhealthy).

Moving on to ultra-flexible humans, the capacity for *identification* and for transfer of identification is almost unlimited. This transferred identification, being 'for' the whole, is crucial to the formation and maintenance of traditional human groups and tribes. With the progressive breakdown of those tribes into the flotsam of mass societies, from the advent of the agricultural revolution onwards, identification *either* transfers back onto the ego-self – as is the case with the hyper-individualism of modern societies *or* transfers onto substitute 'tribes'. Either way the delicate creative interface between natural autonomy and collectivity is damaged or distorted. This displaced identification may range from bizarre forms (such as identifying with a football team on the other side of the world or with the projected image of a pop star) though loyalty to gangs, drugs barons and war lords to the often hysterical mass followings of charismatic populist leaders and tyrants; and beyond this again to the congregations of the great universal faiths that offer meaning to life.

In terms of Convergence – Divergence theory, the majority Convergents – natural followers – more readily transfer loyalty onto groups and causes (which is what they are 'designed' to do of course). For the Divergent minority the position is more complex, with critical judgement brought to bear and a tension between their identification tendency and their stronger egos. This may be resolved by seeking to become lieutenants or even high priests of the movement/cause that they come to identify with.

It should be clear from the above that transferred identification needs to be taken into account in understanding social structure, telling the Social Story. There is also a case for regarding identification with any of the various causes, movements and groups as contagious transmittable memes.

Cultures, Classes, Natios, States and Sub-cultures

The *culture* of a people is what it does together, its practices and beliefs. "Our culture is the framework within which the possibilities of our lives are played out."[39]

Before agriculture and mass society the basic social unit was the hunting group, its size limited by practical considerations. Kindred groups can be simply thought of as tribes (social anthropologists use other terms) and the related tribes as making up a people or **natio**. [The Roman word natio is used since today 'nation' has become synonymous with the state: a control and command structure claiming hegemony over a territory that may include several *natios*, peoples, as well as growing numbers of dis-connected 'cosmopolitan' individuals and waves of more recent immigrants. In passing, the English, Scots, Welsh and (in part) Irish are probably the only non-states recognised as *natios* by the International Football Association.]

In the pre-agriculture period there was normally holarchy [defined here as the situation where power is directly related to responsibility: the true meaning of Divergent leadership.] but sometimes hierarchy [which refers to power pyramids in general] within the scattered hunting groups – but no class structure as such. Class is a by-product of numbers, of social scale, as explored below.

Class

The emergence of class structure derives from three factors: economic, social and cultural.

One of the great insights of Karl Marx[40] was recognition of the importance of **surplus value** in social evolution. For most of pre-history humans lived at subsistence level. There was no surplus to indulge the needs and pretensions of a non-working elite. The birth of agriculture was a decisive moment: giving most of our ancestors a harder, less healthy life (as revealed by bone structure comparisons) but enabling surplus grain etc to be stored as wealth. Since it was now economic to keep slaves who could be worked in the fields on bare subsistence (or even below subsistence) diets, the accumulation of surplus value was now accelerated.

Now it can be argued that the combination of instinctive pecking orders with conscious egos – i.e. the ego as self-image – provided the **social** dimension of class: desire for status and the symbols of status.

Status is a powerful driver in shaping behaviour in both traditional and large state-hierarchic societies, as Veblen[41] in 'The Theory of the Leisure Class' was to show. Even people of moderate wealth may see themselves as poor because they compare themselves with those above them. In England today, status is embodied in both inherited and bought privilege, underwritten by the state.

Whilst Marx exposed the economic basis of class, Friedrich Nietzsche argued the **cultural** component that gave class domination its bitter edge. According to Nietzsche once a people had become 'soft' (in his terms), new 'barbarians' with ruthlessness and energy would come in over the top and install themselves as the new ruling elite[42]. Nowhere was this process more starkly demonstrated than in the invasion of England in 1066 and the brutal subjugation of the English people that was to follow, including of course the 'harrying of the North' and the Norman lord's 'right of the first night' (with the bride).

The critical distinction between socio-economic class – where status superiority can be balanced by a sense of obligation and underlying kinship – and *cultural* class can be summed up in the words *contempt* and *paranoia*. The word villein formerly meant a field labourer, without pejorative connotations. Since our subjection villain has come to its present meaning of a bad, anti-social, untrustworthy person. The paranoia has surfaced repeatedly down the centuries, for example at Peterloo, and has always been there. To quote a line from John Fletcher's essay 'The Secret People': "There is an unbroken line from the paranoid walls of a Norman keep to the Official Secrets Act of today". [43]

Sub-cultures

In modern state-defined rather than culture-defined societies, especially in the era of globalisation, there are few distinct, coherent, un-degraded cultures to point to. Hence the concept of *sub-cultures* becomes relevant.

A ***sub-culture*** may be defined as a section of the larger society that has some identifiable bonds and some values and perhaps practices in common. On this definition a sub-culture can vary in intensity from a pigeon fanciers society (say) through a social group with economic and lifestyle bonds (the dockers and the miners are vivid examples from recent history) to those who, despite differing backgrounds, identify as a natio and may strive to make their commonality tangible – the recent revival of the Cornish language is a case in point. It follows that it is possible to identify with, be embedded in, more than one sub-culture.

Not mentioned so far are those sub-cultures defined by shared faith. Obviously Christian and post-Christian groups such as Catholics, Methodists and Quakers form distinct sub-cultures within broader society, as does the older Pagan tradition. What is significant about the Islamic faith now followed in England is that for some this identity is at least on a par with both natio and state identities. Not since the Middle Ages has this been the case in 'Christian' Europe. Thus a recent immigrant from northern Iraq may identify as a Sunni Muslim first, a Kurd second, an Iraqi third, only functionally as a citizen of a U.K. nation-state and not at all as a recruit to the English natio.

The durability of Jewish culture (the label sub-culture is hardly appropriate) down the ages, despite centuries of oppression and scattering, can probably be attributed to its 'triple lock' of ethnicity* faith and culture (*you can't choose to be a Jew: one criterion is a Jewish Mother).

To speak of values based sub-cultures may seem to be a tautology, since all but the most trivial/functional of sub-cultures must surely hold values in common, not least faith groups and natios. As Nietzsche put it: "every people sets up a table of values over itself".[44] So the notion of values sub-cultures is used in a more restricted sense to define the carriers of new waves of intropy (form changing energy) that can sweep through both social and faith communities and their structures.

These waves usually become spent or accommodated into orthodoxy, but frequently not before they have changed the landscape. Historical examples are the first wave of Islamic expansion out of Arabia, the Puritans in the Reformation, the Bolsheviks in the Russian revolution.

Since the values of these dynamic sub-cultures are transmitted rapidly onto fertile soil under certain conditions, the issue of memes and social types is re-visited below, while values bonding will be taken further in the Ecology and Values Story that follows.

Memes and Social Attitudes

The concept of the meme as a set of ideas and/or values that can be transmitted from one human being to another in a social context has already been made use of in the case of the transfer of self-identity that enables *identification* with a group or tribe.

The meme debate within the scientific community about the detailed mechanisms of person to person transfer, the lack of agreed criteria and definition, the doubtful validity of the comparison with gene transmission and so on, need not invalidate the functional use of the concept in more general social discussion. It has already been noted that *all* category labels break down when examined 'close up'. (e.g. the example of the chiropodist and the size seven foot.)

Although a meme is shorthand for any ideas or values that can be passed on from human to human and thereby replicate themselves throughout a population or sub-culture, it is used below to mean *'**super-memes'**:* world views or unifying myths that shape our attitudes and behaviours while we hold them. How receptive we are to these 'viruses' will depend on both internal factors such as our types and temperaments and external factors: economic circumstances, peer group and cultural influences.

Some (often most) people may be resistant to meme transfer, to new ideas and values. Usually this will be less the case where a major 'climate' shift in views or values is taking place throughout society (or sections of it) and more significant when new, radical or unfamiliar, ideas are being propagated. The author's 1971 Essay[45] (written before either meme theory or Convergence/Divergence principles were generally understood) argued that for any set of ideas under given social conditions there is a *subjective group* able to accept them and that once this group has been saturated further attempts to propagate the ideas will largely fail.

According to Convergent – Divergent theory, Convergents will be more susceptible to propagated memes especially when peer group leaders have endorsed them, since following a lead is part of their social function. On the other hand Divergents can be open to new memes, new world views, that validate their interests and aspirations. In the earlier discussion of social modes it was noted that groups and communities can 'flip' or 'slide' from one mode to another: e.g. 'fair play', 'war communism', 'alienation' etc.

At the level of individuals such a group mode shift requires that at least most members of the group have been receptive to a meme triggered by the new situation and/or conferred by oratory/propaganda. A classic example was the spread of the virus of National Socialism (a form of war communism) in 20s/30s Germany: triggered as much by the humiliation and economic ruin of Germany by the Allies after 'The Great War' as by the persuasive methods of Adolf Hitler.

One attempt to list the *super-memes* or total world views that are competing for our minds and place them in a 'spiral' that is both evolutionary and reflective of the autonomy/collectivity interface is the Spiral Dynamics model: an aspect of the theories developed in the USA by Clare.W.Graves[46] and others. The central portions of this spiral are supported by careful observations of attitudes in one society and contain plausible insights.

However, the extrapolation of the spiral into 'primitive' pre-history and into an 'enlightened' future is questionable and reveals the hidden assumptions of the model as itself a product of the enlightenment meme. Notwithstanding this observation Spiral Dynamics and related attempts at social analysis are worthy of further exploration. The 'four quadrant' model – interior/exterior and individual/collective – has parallels with Jungian and other approaches yet is steadfastly social rather than introspective in its intention.

The attached table [Plate 6] maps SD meme evolution theory in terms of Convergent and Divergent traits.

Plate 6

TYPES AND MEMES

Historical view of Convergent and Divergent behaviours matched to Spiral Dynamics colour Memes

VERY ROUGH TIMELINE (W. EUROPE)	DOMINANT WORLDVIEW of the EPOCH	DIVERGENT MINORITY PRINCIPAL ROUTE TO FULFILMENT/POWER	NEAREST S.D. MEME EQUIVALENT	CONVERGENT MAJORITY PRINCIPAL RESPONSE BEHAVIOURS	NEAREST S.D. MEME EQUIVALENT
10,000 BCE	IMMANENT NATURE	Leadership by Maturity, Moral Courage and Wisdom	NONE	Respect for Elders, Playfulness and Law of Least Effort Satisfaction in Work/Play Cycles Fear of Natural Dangers/Spirits	MODIFIED PURPLE
4,000 BCE	NATURE GODDESSES /GODS				
500 BCE	TRANSCEND-ENTAL GODHEAD	Either: Power by The Sword: Ruthlessness, Courage in Battle Or: Power from Magic/Religion: Dispensing Safety/Salvation	RED	Loyalty, Obedience, sometimes Fanaticism and Scapegoating But also: Satisfaction in Trade or Craft and in Celebrations	STAGE 1 BLUE
1500 CE		Power from Wealth: Trade, Property/Ownership, Labour Surplus Value, Usury (but backed up by The Sword)	ORANGE	Mercenaries, Jobsworths, Moaners, above all Consumers But also: Satisfaction in Socially Valid Work and in Hobbies	STAGE 2 BLUE
1800 CE	RATIONAL OPTIMISM				
During 1900s	RATIONAL PESSIMISM/ CYNICISM	Power from Information: Network Hubs, Control of Flows, Control of Presented Images (but backed up by Ownership Power, and ultimately The Sword) ---------------- Minority: Challenging The System's Vision; Explorations beyond Ego Competition	MOCK YELLOW ---------------- YELLOW	Hyper Consumers: including of Intangibles; Indulgent Therapies and Experiences New Mistrust of Others Sometimes joining New Cults and Protest Movements But also: Trying to maintain The Content of Life via Social Routines	MOCK GREEN
2050?					
THE TIPPING POINT: BREAKDOWN, CHAOS AND CONFUSION					
Future 'A'	FRAGMENTED	New Warlord Terror	RED	Fear, Obedience, Hysteria	BROKEN PURPLE
Future 'B'	HOLISTIC	New Wisdom and Courage: Leaderfulness in Small Groups in an Austerity Environment	MODIFIED CORAL	Work/Relaxation/Celebration Cycles within Co-operative Small Groups in an Austere and sometimes Fearful Environment	MODIFIED TURQUOISE

*   *   *   *   *

Evolution

Evolution happens. In biological evolution the fossil record shows species appearing as distinct creatures, evolving/improving and (usually) ceasing to exist. In the evolution of hyper-cultures or civilizations a similar pattern – from semi-mythical origins to greatness to decay – can be deduced or even observed. Likewise in the evolution of ideas, especially world views or *super-memes*, the same trajectory from maverick emergence to mainstream adoption or even orthodoxy to stagnation and decline may be followed.

The trouble begins when evolution, an intrinsically cyclic process (even galaxies have their life cycles), is mixed up with Enlightenment ideas of linear time and above all *progress*. It is arguably a trait of the human, especially Divergent, ego to want to believe that all previous societies were primitive, that 'we' are the pinnacle and that the future is open to 'our' conquests – an essentially transcendental world view. (Remember, Convergents are much better at immanence, at living the now.) During the twentieth century the Enlightenment world view was increasingly challenged* – but not before it had become deeply embedded in evolutionary theories, whether biological or social.

[*The challenge to Enlightenment optimism/arrogance was anticipated by Nietzsche but really gained impetus with the 'death of optimism' in the First World War trenches and the cutting critiques of the poets, artists and theorists of postmodernism[47]. One may also mention radical thinkers such as Norman O. Brown: "Human history is not a process of becoming wiser but a process of becoming sicker"[48]; a new humility among some scientists; philosophers such as John Gray[49] with his tour de force 'Enlightenment's Wake'; finally the dawning ecological awareness that we are already in the throes of a human induced Sixth Extinction – see Ecology and Values Story below.]

There is still room for debate about the *mechanisms* of evolution. In biological evolution Charles Darwin himself was far less dogmatic about the selection of the fittest among offspring being the only 'improver' than the Neo-Darwinists who claim to be his heirs[50]. Rupert Sheldrake[51], notably in his book 'A New Science of Life' has put forward challenging (and to the guardians of orthodoxy, heretical) arguments for a much more complex and 'intelligent' transmission of genetic information. Richard Leakey and Roger Lewin[52], in 'The Sixth Extinction', argue that in the bigger picture 'luck' – not being in the wrong place at the wrong time – has played a much bigger part than superior qualities in determining who survives. Some recent work suggests that genes *are* capable of acquiring characteristics.[53] Robert Ardrey, in 'The Social Contract'[54] had much earlier pointed out that stotting behaviour – to alert the herd – among Thomson's gazelles has negative survival benefit to the individual. There are many other examples of collaborative or symbiotic behaviour.

None-the-less the sound bites "survival of the fittest" in a nature "red in tooth and claw" have proved enduring – and Darwin has taken the blame. What's more the simplistic notion of progress through evolution has carried over into social improvement schemes. Herbert Spencer[55] was first to suggest that 'selection of the fittest' could be applied to human social evolution, both in physical and cultural terms. This reinforced ideas of human perfectibility in line with Enlightenment progress and was widely influential. It also indirectly popularised eugenics. Despite his extreme individualist outlook aspects of his detailed study of Darwin's new field emphasised the importance of mutuality and co-operation as factors in anthropological evolution.

The consequences of this world view in the following generations ranged from social engineering to improve the stock by eliminating 'the dregs' to less drastic efforts at improving the human mind, or evolving a group mind, through the interaction of leaderful types or other individuals in self-chosen groups. Perhaps the modest aim of enabling less dysfunctional human groups and associations – understanding how types and individuals interact with each other and are influenced by values shifts – could be more focussed without these myths of evolutionary perfection.

Social Mapping (or Space Geography)

Are there ways of showing the limiting options for any large scale society (not small structured group) in terms of its mix of fundamental properties? The 1971 Essay already mentioned attempted this in terms of three parameters, also arguing for a historical transition from a 'blind' or 'unconscious' model applicable to all socially organised creatures to modern 'conscious' (strictly ego-conscious) human societies.

The TSA Triangle

For this purpose it was found that Cartesian co-ordinates were not appropriate. Instead the three fundamental modes argued for – Co-operation, Hierarchy and Competition – were taken as the points of a triangle of possibilities. The core argument was that any real, possible, social organisation could be located within the triangle as some mix of the basic modes. The secondary argument was that the competition mode or corner was inherently unstable except in special time-limited circumstances. Thus in practise real social structures must cluster close to 'the line of no competition' as some mix of hierarchy and co-operation. [Plate 7]

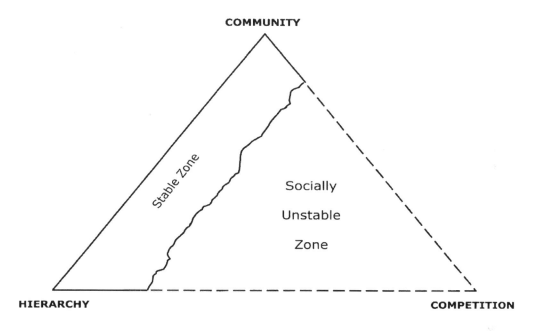

Plate 7

SOCIAL MAPPING: THE TSA TRIANGLE
Insect, Animal and Traditional Human Social Groups

COMMUNITY

Stable Zone

Socially

Unstable

Zone

HIERARCHY

COMPETITION

The next stage of the argument was that modern ego-consciousness transforms the limiting modes such that extreme hierarchy (all power to the centre) becomes Tyranny; extreme competition (within the social organism) becomes Alienation (a concept developed by Marx, Tönnies[56] and others); while the idealistic state of pure co-operation was denoted by the term Sociality. By looking at actual societies it was found that much more of the TSA triangle (as defined above) was 'inhabitable'. Thus mass societies with fairly high levels of alienation (such as ours) could remain stable. [Plate 8]

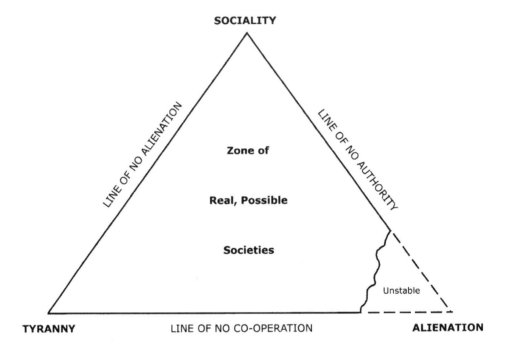

Plate 8

SOCIAL MAPPING: THE TSA TRIANGLE
Modern Large Scale Human Societies

How could this be? To take a small example: in a more cohesive society, if your family house/hut burns down, I and others will naturally rally round and help you to rebuild it. In modern society as we experience it, though certainly not hostile, I am likely to be indifferent (beyond perhaps expressions of sympathy if I am a near neighbour). Yet "I" do rebuild your house. Through my insurance premium, designed to protect *my* house I provide the resources to rebuild yours. This example can be multiplied across all aspects of life. Through similar mechanisms people (us) who do not especially care about each other, perhaps just wanting our wages at the end of the week/month, provide the infrastructure of interdependence that keeps society functioning.

There are likely extremes of alienation that *will* destabilise society: everybody (or most of us) trying to use everybody else for maximum gain. Making money out of money without creating new social wealth is a structural example: investment speculators are probably the pacesetters towards the cliff edge. The warning signs are all around us, from the banking crisis and corruption scandals to the weakening of the formerly very strong ethic of care in the social and health services to the headline making 'senseless' mass killings to the fear in many areas of letting children walk to school or to the nearby park to the almost unremarked fact that humble families who sixty years ago did not bother to lock their doors now have up to three locks on those doors, even in the daylight hours.

These symptoms are reported and mulled over yet the overall social slide towards alienated values is not faced up to as an issue, perhaps because it would challenge all of us and certainly threaten aspects of the 'must grow for ever' market.

Back in 1971 a number of societies were 'located' within the TSA triangle, including in some cases their 'direction of travel'. These positions were/are of course open to debate and would require – at the very least – some agreed criteria for each of the key measures. None the less it is argued that the principle is valid enough to make the TSA triangle a useful starting point for further social mapping.

Plate 9 shows the results of that exercise.

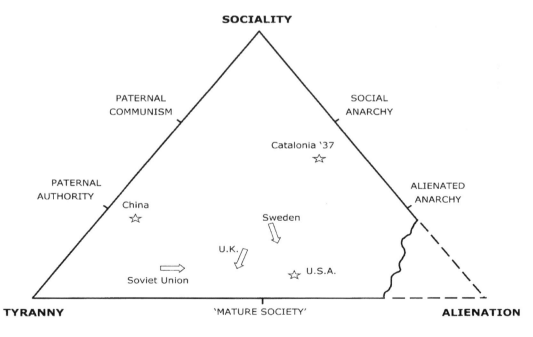

Plate 9

SOCIAL MAPPING: THE TSA TRIANGLE
Mapping Modern States (1971)

Another exercise at the time was to plot the course of the Russian revolution on to the TSA triangle. The result was surprisingly revealing and also in fair agreement with accounts from contemporary sources. [Plate 10]

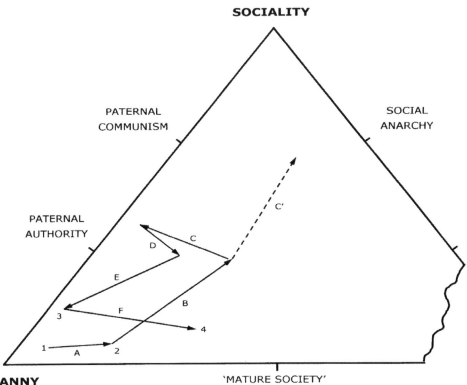

Plate 10

SOCIAL MAPPING: THE TSA TRIANGLE
Charting the Bolshevik Revolution

KEY

1 Czarist Russia before the reform agitation

2 Czarist Russia on the eve of the first revolution

3 Limit of Stalinist oppression

4 1971 estimate

A Concessions made

B Summer 1917 revolution

C' Spontaneous tendency of October revolution

C Bolshevik imposed direction of revolution

D 'New Economic Policy'

E Degeneration of revolution

F 'Normalisation'

Jacobins and Neoliberals

Since that time, the evolution of *Devolve!* out of both community and devolution roots led on to exploration of the relationship – or tension – between the ideal (held by many devolutionists and community activists) of a pluralist civil society and the reality of the modern centralised state. With the aid of a historical perspective the latter was increasingly seen to be underpinned by the ***grand narrative*** of Jacobin philosophy. [Plate 11]

Plate 11

Pluralism and Jacobinism in European history

Rough Dates	PLURALIST THEORY	PLURALIST PRACTICE	JACOBIN THEORY	JACOBIN PRACTICE
~ 350 BCE	Aristotle	N/A	Plato	N/A
0-500 CE		Custom Law beyond Empire	Roman Law Codes	Imperial Rome
500-1000	English Case Law develops from Custom Law	De Facto Confederations of Tribes, Birth of Town Power		
1000-1200	Realist Philosophers: "Associations are Real and should have Legal Rights"	Feudal/Mediaeval Europe	Nominalist Philosophers: "Associations are Fictions"	
1200-1450	ditto (but losing ground)	ditto (but weakening)	Revival of Roman Law	
1450-1550			Machiavelli Luther Calvin	Secular Italian Princes. Henry VII + VIII 'Nationalise' Power in England
1550-1650	Althusius		Bodin Hobbes	Protestant Reformation
1650-1780			Rousseau	(state consolidation period)
1780-1900	Conservative Pluralists: Burke Bonald Liberal Pluralists: Lamennais DeTocqueville Radical Pluralists: Proudhon Kropotkin	Syndicalism (embryonic)	The Messianic Jacobins Marx The Fabians	French Revolution "The People's State" Inheritances: 'Democratic' Totalitarian
1900-1950	Figgis Cole, Laski (for a time) Buber	Guild Socialism (embryonic) Spanish Social Anarchism Early Kibbutzim	Marxism-Leninism	
1950-2011	(Revival of Study of Pluralism)	Birth of Informational and Economic Pluralism	Messianic Neoliberals - towards a global economy	Increasing Centralisation in England: weakening of Local Government, Unions and Functional Autonomies
2012- 2020?	Work to be done!	Internet pluralism?		Global Tensions?
Transition		Ad hoc responses?		Collapsing?

Note that the Pluralist – Jacobin tension cuts across the normally accepted Left – Right polarity, with conservative thinkers and actors such a Edmund Burke on the opposite side of the divide to 'socialist' Fabians such as the Webbs, totally committed to the principle that the State (in the right hands) will deliver for the people.

Because of this focus of *Devolve!* on the relation between human community and the state much less attention had been paid to economic relations as a focus of conflicting forces and as the embodiment of alienation in society. A debt is owed to the Network Project[57] and to Ian Brown in particular for making evident that Alienation – the critical third element in the TSA triangle of social possibilities, symbolised by the market economy – is today increasingly underpinned by the **grand narrative** of Neoliberal philosophy. Also for arguing that since none of the three elements can exist in the pure 'extreme' state, the principle of **accommodation** between any of them is a vital factor in the real politics of real social conditions. These concepts enable a new practical version of the TSA triangle with Civil Society, The State and The Market as its cornices. [Plate 12]

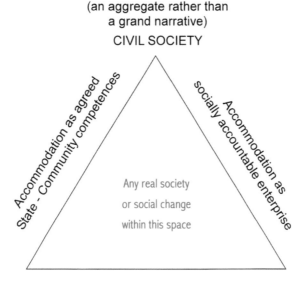

Plate 12

SOCIAL MAPPING: THE TSA TRIANGLE
Grand Narratives: Conflict and Accommodation

Pluralist ideas and values
(an aggregate rather than
a grand narrative)
CIVIL SOCIETY

Accommodation as agreed
State - Community competences

Accommodation as
socially accountable enterprise

Any real society
or social change
within this space

THE STATE
Jacobin philosophy
(historical grand narrative)

Accommodation as
mutual re-enforcement

THE MARKET
Neoliberal philosophy
(historical grand narrative)

Whereas The State and The Market are now seen to have powerful ideological *grand narratives* underpinning them, Civil Society (as an emancipated social-political form) can never be more than an aggregate of pluralist ideals and values. This apparent weakness could become strength in the very different post-transition world anticipated in the next Story.

More Space Geography

The principle of Social Mapping based on limiting conditions, as exampled above with the TSA triangle, may be extended into other fields of enquiry using different parameters.

It is argued that *Space Geography*, already used as a tool in fields of study such as virus mutation, may usefully be applied to animal and human social affairs and attitudes. The critical step is replacing open ended Cartesian parameters with a 'closed space' created by limiting conditions. Three parameter space as used here has the advantage of being quite informative while easily represented on two dimensional paper. However, five parameter modelling (say) of complex social issues can be represented in four dimensions using modern computers.

At the simple end, one dimensional mapping based on only two 'extreme' positions is in common use in social discussion. A clear example is the one dimensional Left - Right model of political views, parties and societies. Hence read-offs such as 'moderate Left' or 'extreme Right'.

As a further application of *space geography*, the tension (and mix) of existential human attitudes to life between *immanence* (living in the now) and *transcendence* (looking towards an infinity point or other world) – as discussed earlier in this story – may be combined with the Nietzschean concept of *excellence** ("a people is merely a diversion by nature to create five or six great individuals") in order to draw an ETI triangle enclosing (at this level) the full range of attitudes to life. [Plate 13] [*See Ecology and Values Story.]

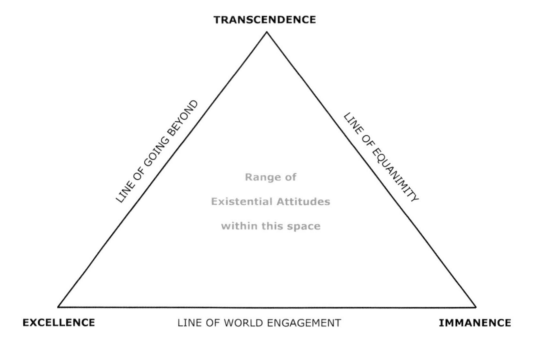

Plate 13

SPACE GEOGRAPHY: THE ETI TRIANGLE
Existential Attitudes To Life

TRANSCENDENCE

LINE OF GOING BEYOND

LINE OF EQUANIMITY

Range of

Existential Attitudes

within this space

EXCELLENCE   LINE OF WORLD ENGAGEMENT   IMMANENCE

Sex and Society

So far in this Story only passing reference has been made to sex, considered by many observers of life – and certainly by most ordinary people – as our most powerful as well as our most problematic instinct or drive (at least when fundamental needs such as for food and security are assured).

How central is the sexual drive? For Freud[58] and his followers the 'life instinct' is synonymous with the sex instinct and all 'life affirming' behaviour is at root sexual. e.g. friendship as aim inhibited sexuality. Yet it is possible to turn this around and to see the sexual drive – though undoubtedly hormone driven – as one possible expression of a broader life energy.

Victor Serge[59] in his book 'Memoirs of a Revolutionary' records that the idealistic and committed young Bolsheviks of 1917 only "re-discovered their sexuality" when the revolution started to turn sour around 1921. In some Eastern wisdoms[60] it is considered possible to move the expression of the life force 'up the chakras' to different levels of interaction with the world, each corresponding to different foci in the central nervous system.

This leads into the broader concept of sublimation – literally 'making sublime'. In social and semi-social creatures this sublimation of instincts and behaviours – including aggression – into ritualised and paradoxical forms is critical to social stability. Konrad Lorenz[61] in his studies of the greylag goose was able to demonstrate this sublimation of behaviours that would otherwise be disruptive within the flock.

In human groups it can be argued that culture as we know it is made possible by sublimated energies, transformed drives, not just in the narrower sense of art and ritual but in most human interactions.

Sexually Affirmative and Sexually Repressive Societies

Sublimation is **not** the same thing as repression. Herbert Marcuse[62], radical social philosopher, introduced the concept *repressive de-sublimation* in examining social control through manipulation of desire. [In effect reversing sublimation into baser instincts for the purposes of social control and economic exploitation.]

Any *healthy* human group must incorporate structures or ground rules that regulate yet permit the natural expression of developing sexual feelings from childhood onwards. It is now accepted by most social anthropologists that so-called primitive societies have in nearly all cases sophisticated arrangements which facilitate the transition to full adulthood.

In contrast almost all large scale 'civilized' societies have built in constraints on, and denials of, sexual expression and natural development, especially of the young: both pre-puberty and post-puberty. This repeats and re-enforces itself in each generation and manifests in ignorance, fear, guilt, hypocrisy; associations of sex with fetishistic, masochistic and sadistic tendencies; projection of these internalised complexes onto publicised 'perverts' by a public always hungry for salacious stories with sexual angles.

Nor has the so-called sexual liberation from earlier taboos resulted in sexual affirmation: in healthy associations entered into with mutual joy, tenderness and respect. Rather it has made sex a 'must have' commodity and sometimes reduced 'the other' to an object. No wonder Norman O Brown[63] could claim: "Human history … is a process of becoming sicker."

This contrast between sexually affirmative and sexually repressive societies was drawn in a critical essay by Dr John Hewetson[64] first published in 1951 and reprinted (with a preface by Colin Ward[65]) in The Raven[66] N° 4 in 1987. In his (doctor's eye view) of the widespread sexual misery he saw around him and in attempts to understand it he drew on the insights of Wilhelm Reich[67] and Bronislaw Malinowski[68]. In 'The Sexual Life of Savages' Malinowski describes the social life of the Tobrian islanders and in particular the freedom of sexual expression afforded to the young, both pre-puberty and post-puberty.

In challenging the vicious circle of sexual repression Dr Hewetson looked to a process of re-education within the structures of society, including anti-natal clinics, schools and universities. In contrast Maureen Boustred[69] in her article 'Towards Human Ecology'[70] argues for semi-autonomous structures featuring a leading role for the young, on the fringes of mainstream society.

Boustred also looks to a study of a traditional society for contrast and inspiration – in this case 'The Muria and Their Ghotul' by Elwin Verrier[71]. The Ghotul as described is both a great house and an institution, organised and lived by the young people with strict codes governing relationships and procedure but with sexual and pre-sexual openness and innocence: "when there is consent and love there is never sin". Elwin observed that pregnancy rates in the Ghotuls were extremely low even though the young women were normally fertile when they moved out and on to permanent adult relationships. Also that there was no delinquency and that venereal disease was unknown.

Looking Forward

Perhaps the key points of relevance to our own values search are not the sexual and quasi-sexual practices as such but the emphasis on openness, honesty and trust coupled with the significant autonomy of young people to collectively self-organise. Plus the affirmation that there is no shame in our natural sexuality.

Could there be any such way forward in our large scale densely populated and stressed societies? The omens are not good, except at the margins. Maureen Boustred herself refers to the beginnings of a ghotul in a relatively isolated park homes site – until it was destroyed by external forces. Another example of an embryonic ghotul pattern – admittedly for limited periods in temporary gatherings – is the Woodcraft Movement[72] with its unisex approach, its strong emphasis on co-operation and on autonomous collective self-organisation (especially of the older age groups) at its camps.

Sex and Civil Society

Is it really this bad for us? Surely most of us cope after a fashion with early hurts and anxieties and grow towards sexual and social maturity? Or do we? The answer, in a society of private lives, is not easy to determine. The answer also partly depends on who 'we' are.

In those communities where there is still some meaningful civil society as a counter-force to the corrosive logic of individualism and alienation; where optimistic assumptions still prevail over cynicism; where there are positive, leaderful role models; where one can find sufficient examples of stable relationships and respect between generations ... then there is hope.

On the other hand, among those broken communities identified by Ferdinand Mount[73] as 'the downers'; in many inner cities and sink estates; among residual collections of people from whom the leaderful Divergents have either absconded in pursuit of advancement or are higher level drug dealers or gang lords; where 'the job', the last connection with dignity and worth, has largely disappeared ... then despair, broken homes, social and sexual dysfunction tend to feed on each other. [Note: John Hewetson wrote from the perspective of a general practice in a deprived area of London but before social alienation and dislocation had reached today's levels.]

Going Deeper

Wilfred Trotter[74], already noted as a formative influence on Braziers, put forward a coherent argument that – in 'herd' animals – the **herd instinct**, in its effect on the behaviour of individuals, is sufficiently powerful to be placed on a par with the 'primary' instincts of food, sex and self-preservation (his triad).

If this is so then this instinct, and its corresponding behaviours, has *emerged* as social group creatures have evolved. It follows that the notion of *emergent properties* with rising levels of biological and social complexity can be extended to drives or patterns that can be called ***emergent instincts***. The nurturing instinct is an example.

Without using the notation of this essay, Trotter makes clear that on the inside of the universe these instinctive behaviours (including herd behaviour) are experienced as self-evidently right, beyond discussion or logical criticism, sometimes rationalised so as to appear defensible.

Continuing from the Natural World Story, Sixth Pattern. From the inside of the universe the brain may be viewed as an epiphenomenon of the processes of the mind – a wart on the crusty surface! Still conforming to neurological understanding of course: all credit to Apollonian science. And still a party to reciprocal interaction.

Staying with the inner, experiencing, side of the universe, most of us would accept that love – for example – is not the same thing as sex. In the Freudian view (as noted above) love, and even friendship, are merely sublimations of the sexual drive. There are at least two other possibilities. One is that love for the other, seeking completeness in and with the other, is the experiencing side of an emergent instinct of bonding with obvious advantages for child rearing in complex animals where the young take a long time to mature.

A second possibility is that the yearning that many of us have experienced is an aspect of something more fundamental than that. A feature or even a pattern of our universe, seeking against all obstacles and impossibilities for completeness with the other (or others). Thus the readiness of simple, lighter, 'lonelier' atoms such as hydrogen to undertake thermo-nuclear transformation with intropy release (all yearning is stored intropy) into heavier elements may be another example of this same pattern that we are privileged to know (no metaphors in nature, remember).

Yet all good things come up against the second threshold of Ivan Illich. In human affairs 'threesomes' are rare: even more difficult to keep stable over time than bonded pairs. In atomic physics heavier elements consume more intropy than they release and beyond Lead they are always unstable: subject to radioactive decay (as are 'unbalanced' isotopes of some common elements).

Throughout nature, both functional and dysfunctional variations abound. Homosexual behaviour seems to be fairly constant at about 7% across a wide range of gregarious animals[75], so is not un-natural – though it may be *socially* destabilising in *some* cultures and natios (in modern cosmopolitan mass societies there is not much left to destabilise).

In contrast many other patterns, from the shallowness of many relationships in mass societies through to objectivism and fetishism, may be considered dysfunctional. As already noted above, to Herbert Marcuse they represented *repressive de-sublimation* of our natural socialised instincts.

Many of the propositions in this section remain speculative and open to challenge: work to be done in knowing ourselves in order to form functional and stable human groups after the changes. What is not in doubt is that the discipline of social psychology is very much in its infancy – and likely to remain so as long as its explorers cling to the life rafts of objectivity and fear to strike out, naked, on the inside of the universe.

Summary

It has been argued that to have some understanding of the Social Story – how and why human social structures function, malfunction and fail – a number of notions or concepts are necessary tools. Among the key concepts identified: -

The Creative Interface between Autonomy and Collectivity.

Social Modes: 'Fair Play'; 'War Communism'; 'Alienation'; 'Get You Back'; 'Anarcho Panic'.

Social Types: Convergents and Divergents; Resistives and Sensitives.

Organic Democracy; Divergent Arenas.

Immanence and Transcendence.

Identity and Identification.

Culture, Sub-culture and Class.

Tribes, Natios, States.

Memes, Modes, Moods.

Social Mapping … Space Geography.

Hierarchy, Competition, Co-operation … Tyranny, Alienation, Sociality.

Jacobin and Neoliberal grand narratives; Accommodation.

Sexual Affirmation and Sexual Repression

Herd Instinct, Emergent Instincts.

CHAPTER 3

The Ecology and Values Story

Why link ecology and values? It is argued here that ecology, taken seriously, has to imply a change of standpoint; a re-consideration of goals or purposes for those humans becoming aware of its dimensions. And in the Natural World Story it was argued that morality, value, "what is right to do" is not absolute but is relative: determined by the situation and the purpose seeking attainment.

* * * * *

Karl Marx, in a letter to Engels as early as 1870, said: "England's Proletariat is the World's Bourgeoisie". This insight was so stunning that its implication should have taken the interlocking model of Marxist social theory back to the drawing board. At the very least a *recognition* that the peasant classes of the world, by virtue of their condition, had potential as engines of revolution or attempted revolution when certain triggers were in place (as was to happen in Russia, China, Indonesia and other locations) ... coupled with a *recognition* that, by virtue of their growing stake in the system, the 'advanced' industrial working classes (both the leaderful Divergents and the followful Convergents) could soon be bought off from whatever revolutionary intent they may have had – as was to happen in England, Wales and Scotland despite the 'near miss' of 1919.

Now the women and men toiling in the sweatshops and factories of 1870 could be forgiven for not knowing their 'bourgeois' status. Yet compared to their parents condition in 1830 (say) they had already come a long way – due partly to the achievements of organised labour, including its culture building dimension

(Ferdinand Mount[76] in 'Mind The Gap' pays generous tribute), partly to restraining legislation on unbridled exploitation (e.g. the Truck Act), partly to the 'reaching down' of the outputs of productive wealth – including social infrastructure – beyond the middle classes. This of course included wealth pouring in from the colonies. And it might be added that some people of adequate means and position were willing to become 'traitors to their class' by supporting the cause of labour: William Morris was a notable example[77].

What has all this got to do with ecology? Today, almost 150 years later, we know enough to recast the original insight: "The World's teeming humanity is the Planet's Bourgeoisie".

To the millions, billions, across the globe struggling to exist on less than two dollars a day, beset by global market wealth extraction, density and greed driven inter-group conflict and brutality, natural and human induced climate disasters ... their position as privileged exploiters of the planet is no more clear to them than was that of those 1870s mill workers.

Yet human population continues to *increase* while other species, other components of our ecosystem, continue to vanish and disintegrate at a staggering rate – the Sixth Extinction is for real and happening now, as Richard Leakey and Roger Lewin[78] have argued in the book of that name. Alongside this the human culture web of diverse cultures and languages is being destroyed in a parallel catastrophe.

Even if human population levels off at nine billion by 2050 (as some predict) and later falls back to seven or six billion, it is a core axiom of this essay – not provable as science yet reasonable as wisdom – that this would still leave *one hundred times too many people* for a realistic chance of halting and reversing the Sixth Extinction in due course. Now, if any other species than humans were the cause of this destruction – say locusts – then this sort of statement would hardly be controversial.

Environmentalism and Ecology

No mention of consumption? Especially the now massive consumption of relatively small numbers in the 'rich' world? At this point we need to make a critical distinction between Environmentalism and Radical Ecology.

Environmentalism can be said to be rooted in the Western liberal tradition. [Ironically the same tradition that produced the rational Enlightenment, free trade, eventually the Neoliberal ideology and economic juggernaut. Note, for instance, the two faces of Adam Smith as humanist and economist.[79]] Today at least a sizeable minority of those of us who feel that we can afford to be so *are* environmentalists. It is taken as read that we are looking at ways to change aspects of our personal consumption (though often not our incomes: the measure of our total impact). We may join various action campaigns and Transition groups.[80] We may also lobby governments to change pollution and consumption priorities. We may even sign up to Population Matters[81] with its "stop at two (children)" campaign. The point here is that we can hold these purposes; strive for these goals, within the context of our *existing* human liberal morality and values.

Radical Ecology is something different again. If the thesis laid out above is correct; if we are convinced of the Sixth Extinction and its cause, then we are called on to be 'traitors to our class' (humanity) and side with Gaia, with the proles of the ecosystem: with the marine and land based creatures, with the insects, with the trees and plants. As James Lovelock[82] puts it:

"I see myself as a kind of shop steward for all the rest of the life on the planet apart from people. I feel that I have to be because there is nobody else speaks for them. They don't have any representation."

This 180° shift, this radical change of purpose, requires a new moral attitude, new values – scary as hell. Who will be the warriors for this cause? Let us first distinguish between *values radicals* and *values warriors*.

Values radicals in general may be defined as: "persons aiming to move the 'centre of gravity' or median attitude of a group, people or society towards their values, to achieve a values shift". There are many examples. Indeed the whole of cultural history can be seen as on-going struggles around values.

Now these tensions have always previously been *within* the Social Story – in modern terms around such key notions as *mutuality, caring* and *humility* versus opposing concepts of *individuality, aspiration* and *arrogance*.

Going beyond the human story, *values warriors* may be defined as: "persons aiming to encourage values shift (in a proportion of any group, people or society) from a homocentric stance to an ecocentric stance" In other words the struggle takes on a new dimension: one between *all* human-centred purposes and the broader eco-centric purpose: the needs of Gaia as a dynamic integrative system embracing all creatures in our biosphere. As radicals challenging homocentric assumptions we now dare to claim the title.

Only after 'the deluge' will the two aspects of values struggle converge among survivors: humble respect for our planet and social nurturing of each other will accord once human numbers are suitably modest.

What, if anything, we might actually *do* to start working with Gaia; start re-balancing our planet – what the options are – will be considered later. For the moment let us talk values.

Holders of the new values, carriers of this life stance, will know themselves as partners with Gaia. This will be true not only before the 'cataclysm' or 'adjustment' (take your pick) but after it. If our values warriors, or rather their memes, do not survive and spread in sufficient numbers then even a chastened humanity may revert to the same human centred 'more is better' values that have caused the Sixth Extinction now upon us.

A great responsibility rests on the shoulders of Divergents among values warriors in this century. As work with Chicago street gangs in the 1920s demonstrated[83], in a situation where the writ and norms of the state are weak or non-existent (as they often will be) then one leaderful person can 'swing' maybe twenty Convergents. The weakness, as ever, may lie in Divergent rivalries: the ego problem is far from solved. It is suggested that work in this area – calling on tools and wisdom already available – is one of *three* mountains we have to climb.

The second task sounds simple enough: co-operation within the tribe or new-formed group (there may be no cities). Recent work linking mental processes with social interactions, including the discovery of mirror neurones[84], suggests that empathy and sufficient co-operation within the settlement or roving band should come naturally (note also the 'fair play' mode in the Social Story above). So why doesn't it?

Reducing complex interactions to 'primary' factors we might identify some reasons. Ego domination was discussed in the Social Story and listed above. 'Untimely' responses to accumulated past hurts are recognised and challenged in certain therapies and counselling groups[85]. Some may need this help: most of us need to remember to nurture each other through positive 'strokes'. Again, in modern society population density and/or resource scarcity can make us feel threats to each other, *be* threats to each other. In the lower population density contemplated the next 'village' may be a day's walk away. Humans will value each other again.

Strengthening community bonds can start now. A dramatic reduction in human numbers during this century has been indicated. Yet in one respect there is a need to *increase* the numbers: not of individuals but of distinct tribes and cultures. This vital diversity – the human culture web – has parallels with the biological ecosystem. Like the ecosystem it is also under threat from global monoculture. So both protecting and re-creating bonded tribes and natios, even among the English, will be on the agenda – is now on the agenda.

Once we, or our successors, have addressed these issues; once there are vibrant, dispersed clans and tribes with social wisdom and nurturing skills, the conditions for un-neurotic social modes such as *fair play* will be met, even in fraught physical conditions.

Revaluation of Values

The third challenge will be the hardest: the "revaluation of all values". The problem is on two levels: biological and cultural. Considering our deep biological instincts first, the purpose and morality of every species, population, tribe, culture is to survive and propagate: "go forth and multiply" is a moral command. This has been essential for humans, no less than other organisms. The historical or rather anthropological reality has been existence at or near Ivan Illich's first threshold (see the Natural World Story above). Most forms of life have eventually fallen below this threshold and ceased to exist, including our human cousins the Neanderthals.

So when humans ... the most successful hunters, gatherers, fabricators, communicators of all time ... start hitting the second threshold, start devouring their environment, the *necessary reversal* of the purpose and morality of 'survival at all costs' is utterly daunting – even for an animal 'programmed not to be programmed' to the extent of creating and transmitting paradoxical memes.

As if this challenge were not enough for even the most committed of values warriors, there is the cultural overlay of liberal morality, an aspect of what Nietzsche called slave morality (which he traced to the Judaeo-Christian tradition:

"the meek shall inherit the Earth" ... (after the revolution) "the workers will seize power").

Alongside widespread belief in an afterlife (Valhalla in the Pagan tradition) most natural peoples were stoical and pragmatic about death. They saw that individual human life *was* cheap and often saw death for the tribe as an honour and a duty – not just in battle. In social anthropology the examples of the elderly (expensive to feed) Inuit cutting themselves adrift on an ice flow and the 'past sell by date' Polynesian paddling out into the open sea on a one way journey are well known.

One of the most negative features of liberal morality is its individualism: valuing the individual ego above the group, the natio, the cause, the whole. Indeed not even being able to comprehend the whole as a living organism contributing to diversity. The utilitarian maxim "the greatest good of the greatest number" has simply no concept of forms of life beyond individuals. [Note: this criticism is not an argument for blind collectivism, least of all for mass collectivism hijacked by a despot's ego]. It was noted in the Social Story that organic structured human groups (in normal mode) exist on the *creative interface* between individual (or family) autonomy and group interdependence and co-operation. Further, Such groups exist as organisms with more complexity (and longer lifespans) than their individual members.

Since today liberal morality sets itself up as the defender of timeless universal values it is worth reminding ourselves how era specific and (Western) hyper-culture specific it was and is. In the coming era of necessary change its core mantra that "all human life is precious" will pose a direct threat not only to the total ecosystem, not only to the potential role of any surviving human groups as partners with nature, but to the structure, values and existence of those groups. Furthermore its second mantra of the denial of excellence and differing roles: "all human beings are created equal" has the potential to undermine a social fabric based on the leaderful – followful dynamic just at the point when the great central states are dissolving.

By default the field will be left open to warlords, drugs barons and the like. In contrast, where attitudes that support social structure based on complementary roles are widespread, the formation of small and viable groups, natios, societies will be enabled.

In view of this scathing attack on liberal morality it is only fair to acknowledge its contribution (in its formative years) in breaking down hegemonic and tyrannical certainties, encouraging doubt and questioning, promoting tolerance of different views, the co-existence of different memes ... as a real contribution to diversity. However, as liberal morality became the new orthodoxy it became the new tyranny. Political correctness is perhaps a trivial example. Of more consequence has been its effect in for many years largely silencing the population debate, arguably costing both humanity and the planet almost half a century of precious time.

Another aspect of this orthodoxy (revealing its Jacobin roots) has been its endorsement of cosmopolitan, fragmented individuals mediated by the state. William Cobbett[86], the last of the pre-Jacobin radicals, understood real people, real sufferers, knew the value of community and dignity in the world then being taken apart by 'progress'. Karl Marx commented that Cobbett "looked for popular liberty rather in the past than in the future". What neither Marx nor Thomas Payne nor any of the radical Jacobins could comprehend was that the Enlightenment future was a road to nowhere.

Yet another feature of cosmopolitan liberal morality has often been vitriolic hostility against defenders and proponents of traditional cultures and natios, including the English. George Orwell observed (not an exact quotation)[87] that England is probably the only example in the world where the intellectuals are ashamed rather than proud of their culture and heritage. The paradoxical result of the orthodoxy that it is 'not nice' or even 'fascist' to defend English culture (or Welsh culture etc) has been that the field has been left open to actual chauvinists and bigots: consigning the issue to the fringes.

It follows from this last point that an important part of nurturing the co-operative values that we will eventually need to survive in the troubled future is renewed attention to – and support for – those cultures and regional sub-cultures that are, for many of us, our heritage and birth right, together with empathy and political support for engulfed and suppressed peoples across the planet. This last aspect is critical for maintaining the diversity of our human culture-web.

Our Values

So what purpose defines our values? Sounds easy if you say it quickly: ***"To defend the entire ecosystem and its diversity against all partial interests and limited moralities"*** As the daughter of the great paleo-anthropologist Richard Leakey is reported to have said: "If it was a choice between preventing the death of my own father and preventing the death of the last breeding tiger ... I would choose the tiger."

The values contrast may be posed as a question. Does Gaia – the living planet – exist for humanity? Is it our life support system? Or does our species exist for Gaia? Is it a small, ultimately transient yet valuable contribution to its magnificent diversity? If the former then a human population of perhaps two billion might be sustainable in the medium term in a human managed less diverse environment.. If the latter then a population of say sixty million (still far higher than any other great ape) could be envisaged as a credible limit for maximum diversity and richness of all life, without a distorting human impact. [The simple concept of total population has been used above. More relevant to real creatures is local population *density*, both in terms of filling ecological niches and the stability or meta-stability of social groups and social behaviour modes.]

It is one thing to know a difficult course of action in the head, quite another to follow it with the heart and to face it in the gut. Below even the pervasive meme of liberal morality, for some of us well embedded in our psyches, lie our deep homocentric instincts – defend the human, defend me! Perhaps the key qualities we need for the task of grasping and advocating these different values are wisdom and courage, plus of course mutual encouragement from each other.

Superman?

We have already mentioned Friedrich Nietzsche as a lodestar for new values: the first values warrior. His wisdom can take us part of the way on our journey. His writings, from the poetic 'Thus Spake Zarathustra' to 'On the Genealogy of Morals' (now considered his most important work) undertake a complete demolition of the foundations of liberal morality and egalitarian democracy. No wonder he was considered "mad, bad and dangerous to read". He remains challenging and troublesome, as well as inspiring, to this day. Of significance to us is that he wrote from passion, from the gut, despite a brilliant mind.

Elitist, sexist but not racist or chauvinist, his aim in "the revaluation of all values" was not, in his time, to replace a homocentric with an ecocentric morality but to replace a decadent morality (already, as he thought, sliding into nihilism) with the morality of the new leaderful man, defining his own morality out of his purposes.

Nietzsche did not have the concept of the **complementary** relationship between Divergent (leaderful) and Convergent (followful) types, each bringing something to the table ... so he could only uphold his new aristocrats, his new warriors, at the expense of denying value to the herd, to the 'small people'.

Nietzsche looked to his supermen beyond what he saw as the present era of mediocrity. Yet this was an overcoming in the real world. He stood on the side of immanence and opposed "any form of transcendence, whether moral or divine, ...saying that transcendence drove one to slander this world and this life."[88]

Although anticipating the future in many ways Nietzsche had no concept of human arrogance in nature , of humans running amok in nature.

We too are values warriors. Who shall we choose as our super-hero, our representative? Why not the humble woodlouse – an icon of immanence? Doing its thing, doing its number, for hundreds of millions of years while entire species, let alone civilisations, rose and fell.

Zarathustra says: "I teach you the Superman (Ubermensch). The Superman is the meaning of the Earth. Let your will say: 'The Superman *shall* be the meaning of the Earth' ". Yet we values warriors would have Zarathustra say: "I teach you the woodlouse. The woodlouse is the meaning of the Earth. Let your will say: 'The woodlouse *shall* be the meaning of the Earth' ".

On the other aspect of the new wisdom, understanding and arguing for the beauty, the majesty and the fragility of our ecosystem and also our dependence on it, the likelihood of "Gaia's Revenge" for what we have already done to it ... much work has already been done for us by brave and wise pioneers such as James Lovelock and Richard Leakey[89]. Had we ears to hear, the message was already clear one hundred years earlier from the wisdom of indigenous peoples:

> "Only when the last tree has died and the last river been poisoned and the last fish been caught......will we realise that we cannot eat money." – *Cree Proverb*

We will need courage too! In challenging head-on the belief of our fellow humans in the value and rightful dominance of humanity, in their right to life in as many numbers as may be ... we shall face disbelief, derision, hostility and worse. We may lose most of our friends. We shall certainly gain enemies. In face of these challenges, beyond the psychic strength of most of us alone, bonding around these values will be essential. The values warriors of the dark times will need to form a cohesive sub-culture in order to bear and transmit the tasks.

It is worth stepping back to remind ourselves of the *three* tasks that it has been argued be in our sights:

♦ Seeking tools for challenging or handling the (Divergent) ego.
♦ Addressing the various blocks to social co-operation and empathy in small groups.
♦ Exploring all aspects and implications of the shift to an eco-centric morality.

Although intended to prepare the ground – propagate the value – of good humility *after* the anticipated transition, much of the work towards co-operation and partnership is valid in its own right, for *the now*, and will remain so even if the forecasts and assumptions of this essay are wrong.

We need to find each other *now* in order to clarify, modify, our tentative initial understandings (of which this essay will merely be one), merge them into other similar thinking doubtless on-going in various hearts and minds. ***A prime purpose of this essay is to send out a signal that may be picked up by potential values warriors,*** rather than to convince others (coming to the issues from different perspectives) of its arguments.

Independent, freethinking centres and communities will be important to the work. Braziers School of Integrative Social Research (which has in part inspired this essay) examples such an educational community.

Action?

Assuming that some proportion of humanity comes to recognition of the need for a Radical Ecology that goes beyond Environmentalism, what are the options? Before proposing some it is necessary to deal with the "it's all too late" viewpoint.

In one sense it is already too late, too late for the tens of thousands of species already extinct or about to be extinct. The Sixth Extinction is well under way. It will also be too late to reverse any major changes to the hospitability of our planet to life. Yet unless we believe (as does philosopher John Gray[90]) that there will be *no* human survivors by (say) the year 2100 then we have a responsibility, just through being aware, to do what we can to pick up the pieces, to get wise, to work towards preventing the Seventh Extinction.

So, assuming some human survival, what are the possible (though maybe not all achievable) courses of action? As values warriors, not embarrassed by reactions from liberals or other values standpoints, we should attempt to consider all possible options – however "mad, bad or dangerous" – under the general heading of Radical Ecology. Some of these are offered here (the list may not be exhaustive):

- Do nothing; let nature take its course.
- Escape to another planet.
- Environmental action only.
- Ecological action by example, encouragement and meme transfer (changed values climate).
- Eugenics.
- Population step change – centimation.

Note that the latter alternatives do imply the over-riding by some humans of the life prospects of other humans. In the early options things will still happen to us but Gaia herself will be the agent.

Considering these: -

The *first* alternative is also the most likely: that there will be no concerted human will for Radical Ecology. In what Lovelock calls "Gaia's revenge" the feedback loops of the ecosystem will provoke the population crash first predicted by the Club of Rome[91] around 1970 ('Limits to Growth' 1974) – see their 'no corrective action' computer simulation attached. [Plate 14] In fact the death rate to birth rate precipice would almost certainly be more severe than that shown as their modelling only took into account physical factors such as resources and pollution, not social and psychic breakdown, brutal resource conflicts and desperate scavenging of remaining biomass. Further, there was no attempt to evaluate the effect on other species in our biosphere.

The *second* option – escape to another planet – is included because it is mooted by a surprising number of people as the solution to our problems. On best information, the technology to create a self-sustaining colony for even a modest number of humans on (say) the moon is still several decades away. The odds against relocating even some of Earth's teeming millions to some new paradise in any foreseeable future are – well – astronomical. Even if this were possible, the thought of letting un-redeemed Homo sapiens loose on the rest of the galaxy is frightening!

Plate 14

THE LIMITS TO GROWTH – Report for The Club Of Rome – 1971 – Standard Assumptions Model

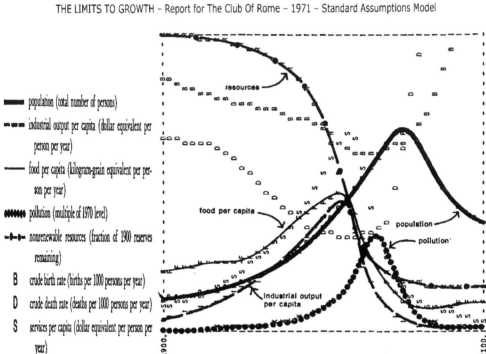

population (total number of persons)

industrial output per capita (dollar equivalent per person per year)

food per capita (kilogram-grain equivalent per person per year)

pollution (multiple of 1970 level)

nonrenewable resources (fraction of 1900 reserves remaining)

B   crude birth rate (births per 1000 persons per year)

D   crude death rate (deaths per 1000 persons per year)

S   services per capita (dollar equivalent per person per year)

The "standard" world model run assumes no major change in the physical economic, or social relationships that have historically governed the development of the world system. All variables plotted here follow historical values from 1900 to 1970. Food, industrial output, and population grow exponentially until the rapidly diminishing resource base forces a slowdown in industrial growth. Because of natural delays in the system, both population and pollution continue to increase for some time after the peak of industrialization. Population growth is finally halted by a rise in the death rate due to decreased food and medical services.

The **third** course, vigorous environmental action by both individuals and governments, is the one being acted on and argued for by an increasing and increasingly concerned minority at this time (2011). The Club of Rome did a whole series of further computer simulations [Plate 15] making various assumptions of reduced pollution or/and increased available resources (which latter could be achieved by better conservation, by increased use of renewables or by new 'finds'). The scary result was that the death/birth crossover was simply postponed while human population rose further. (The fact that better data is now available on population, resources, pollution etc does not compromise the core message of 'Limits to Growth').

This delay to any major reduction in biomass consumption and habitat destruction would mean that species extinction rates and consequent biodiversity reduction would continue at very high levels for longer. The apparently paradoxical result that looms into view is that ***environmental action alone will actually accelerate the Sixth Extinction,*** leading to a still bleaker future. Turning this point around, unchallenged short term consumption levels will *bring forward* the human population peak and intensify the subsequent collapse, lifting more of the burden of humanity from our ecosystem.

Plate 15

THE LIMITS TO GROWTH – Report for The Club Of Rome – 1971 – Better Assumptions Model

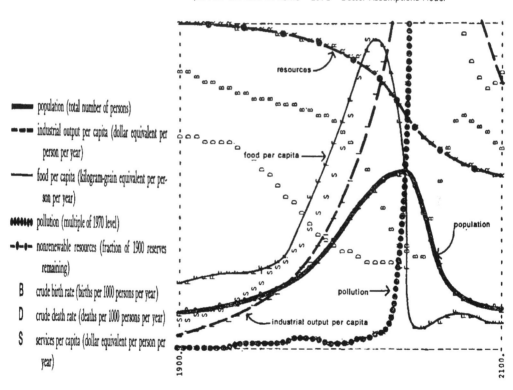

population (total number of persons)

industrial output per capita (dollar equivalent per person per year)

food per capita (kilogram-grain equivalent per person per year)

pollution (multiple of 1970 level)

nonrenewable resources (fraction of 1900 reserves remaining)

B crude birth rate (births per 1000 persons per year)

D crude death rate (deaths per 1000 persons per year)

S services per capita (dollar equivalent per person per year)

To avoid the food crisis of the previous model run, average land yield is doubled in 1975 in addition to the pollution and resource policies of previous figures. The combination of these three policies removes so many constraints to growth that population and industry reach very high levels.

Although each unit of industrial production generates much less pollution, total production rises enough to create a pollution crisis that brings an end to growth.

There is a need to qualify these provocative statements. First, the assumptions that underpin this essay could simply be *wrong* – and the stakes are high. Second, assuming that they are *not* wrong, the strategies of encouraging co-operative endeavour and a less cavalier attitude to nature, more humility before nature, go some way towards propagating the values that survivors into the future will need. Third, if they *are* wrong these same activities remain valid in their own right.

Radical Solutions

The next three possible ways forward, attempts to raise the death rate before Gaia does it for us, enter the realm of Radical Ecology with the values shift away from the human centred (preservation of life) standpoint noted above. (Why not concentrate on lowering the birth rate? This could form part of an overall strategy but the scope would be limited without skewing the age profile to such an extent that it would threaten the viability of those groups surviving into a post-transition era.)

Values Reversal

Among these, the fourth suggested approach – a small minority of values warriors arguing for a new emphasis on the ecosystem rather than one species, for group rather than individual survival, for a new attitude to life and death, plus being willing to 'walk the talk' with their own lives – would seem to be spitting in the wind rather than a serious strategy.

This does not take into account the power of super memes to change the values climate across entire cultures to the extent that value systems initially confined to fringe minorities come to be embedded in large minorities or even majorities within that culture. The work of Spiral Dynamics[92] researchers in demonstrating these major values shifts in one culture has been mentioned. We also noted the role of Divergents in giving a lead to others, helping to accelerate a values shift. It is at least conceivable that future humans will know and value their place in nature, will understand that they should not take more than their share, will regard it as madness to spoil a full life by ending it with years of decline and possibly pain while denying both their children and other creatures their place and time. "Did people once want to live for ever, Mummy?"

Eugenics

The fifth possible road forward could not pose a bigger contrast to the above. In the early years of the last century, influenced by the Social Darwinism of Herbert Spencer[93] (who coined the phrase "survival of the fittest") eugenics was a proper subject for discussion and advocated by a wide range of 'social engineers' – it must be said with elitist or even snobbish implications in many cases.

There have been genocidal holocausts before and since but the practical application of eugenics in the heart of Europe by the German Third Reich was to take it off the agenda for generations.

The elimination of twenty million 'social impurities' was carried out with the aim of creating a 'pure' German stock rather than any criteria of social worth or social loyalty. (Jews, communists, trade unionists, gays, gypsies, and so on went to the gas chambers. Even Protestants such as Pastor Niemöller were imprisoned and narrowly escaped execution.) The powerful emotional impact of that holocaust[94] has obscured recognition of the *failure* of the project as eugenics and silenced debate over what criteria (if any) could be justified in any circumstances. Humans practice eugenics on other species all the time, so presumably we could not complain if wise dolphins (say) had the power to do it to us.

Eugenic action could in principle result in drastic population reduction and arrest the Sixth Extinction. The unanswered questions are who could/should have the authority (and the means) to 'wield the knife' and by what criteria should the decisions be made? Even 'preserving the excellent' (however defined) is challenged by understanding the complementary nature of human social relations.

Centimation

Is there another road to drastic, swift, population reduction? Probably several, all elitist by implication in that some person or persons does it to us. The example that could be given here is the 99% virus: lethal in that proportion to humans but not harming any other species. The chief merit of this form of Radical Ecology is that it immediately lifts the mass burden of humanity from our ecosystem, arrests the Sixth Extinction and (after some overshoot) allows a gradual recovery as available niches are filled by first plants and then animals.

Other features are that the horror, though terrible, would be short lived; that the centimation would not discriminate – so no eugenics or skewing of age or gender population balances; that the resulting very low human population density is one of the required conditions for less stressed more co-operative human groups (see above). It is an open question whether the meme(s) of ecological stewardship and social co-operation would be dispersed in sufficient numbers among the survivors to form a credible proportion of values warriors – that depends in part on the work we do now to find each other and propagate to other receptive minds.

Conditions would be appalling at first, many people traumatised. However, the relative abundance of natural resources plus slowly declining pollution should ensure good prospects for stabilisation and a new partnership with nature among the dispersed human groups. Unlike James Lovelock our 'new traditional people' might feel no regrets for the passing of "civilisation and its discontents".

Could it be done? Almost certainly. Persons unknown may be working on the project even now for all we know[95]. Then again, through the lottery of random virus mutation, nature may take matters into her own hands as part of what Lovelock has called "Gaia's revenge".

Should it be done? It cannot be the role of this exploratory essay into integrative theory to make judgements between courses of action (or inaction) ahead of broader dialogues and wider wisdom. The modest aim is to lay out (some of) the roads to the future and perhaps to note the likely effects of each as far as they may be foreseen. Among the criteria in comparing choices, the foremost must be both the likelihood that each one of them could happen and, if it did, how rapidly it might halt and reverse the Sixth Extinction on planet Earth. Not far behind would be the values mix of the survivors: the prevalence of values such as humility before nature; being immanently in and of the world; knowing responsible participation as the price of empowerment; valuing partnership between and among both leaderful and followful humans; respecting autonomy and difference in a framework of necessary co-operation; seeking fulfilment in the cycles and struggles of life.

Overview

One way to compare strategies is by way of a chart or table. [Plate 16] It will be obvious that there are so many assumptions that any 'outcomes' can only have comparative value at best or at least enable discussion to move forward. For the population crash (death rate over birth rate ratio) the Club of Rome computer runs probably remain the best starting point.[96]

Plate 16

ACTIONS TO ADDRESS THE SIXTH EXTINCTION

Estimated Comparative Effects

Strategy	Comment on strategy	% Prospect of being main change agency	Human Population drop from peak by 2100	Possible modified 6th Extinction – 'units'	Post transition rating of relationships (0 to 10)	Comment on rating
Do nothing	Gaia does the crash	35%	95%	100 (reference)	2	Dog eat dog scramble in final stages?
Mass migration to another planet	Assumes 10% to stay	<<1%	90%	60?	3??	Business as usual attitude?
Strong environmental action	Birth rate action, light footprint, best techno.	20%	40%	120**	6	'Living lightly' stewardship of nature
Values shift to ecocentric stance	99% target not reached by 2100	15%	90%	70	8	Ecocentric partnership with nature
Eugenics	Depends who does it to us and their aims	10%	95%	55	5??	'Authoritarian' stewardship?
Centimation – step change in population	By virus or other means	20%	99%	50*	4	Could be better if eco-values prevalent among survivors
		Adding up to 100%				

**More damage to biosphere due to delayed population step change!　　*Even this drastic step too late for many. Extinction already under way.

Note: All figures unreliable due to complex assumptions – main purpose is to provoke thought.

Conclusion

As for the broader dialogues, this essay has from the start been an invitation and a call to values warriors as now defined to share their concerns, their wisdom and their purpose.

It has been argued that humans have become over-successful as a species – greatly exceeding the second threshold of balance with the biosphere. They have developed cleverness without wisdom, thereby sawing off not just the branches on which they sit but the very trees of life.

Two possibilities for a rebalanced biosphere are implied. Gaia, with or without the help of some humans, brings human population down to numbers comparable with the other great apes. And some humans (values warriors) strive for maximum proportions of the deep values of humility before and co-operation with nature among survivors of what is to come.

End Note

The three Stories of this essay have been written in general terms, making observations on and arguments from both the inside and the outside of the universe. Certainly not dispassionate: motivated understanding; relative to purpose, to outcomes, to a particular morality – yet still in general terms.

There is now a need to become personal, to use 'i' (preferring lower case in mid-sentence as a small ego challenge). I am writing this at the age of seventy-five after a life in the privileged 'first' world with fairly good health, much joy, some woe (mostly inflicted by my own ego), certainly a gradually growing fulfilment. As a values warrior i am beginning to pass the baton. Although i am not deaf to the arguments of friends and comrades, my provisional decision is to exit the planet, to melt back into the Universe, at the age of eighty. Of course Weird[97] – fate – may have its own plans for me.

By then i shall perhaps have lived too long, adding to the numbers; will certainly have consumed far more than my share of the planet's resources; be hoping that my contribution – basically relaying the wisdom so many others have taught me – repays some of this debt.

For how could i even hint that some of us should lay down our lives for our ecosystem, for Gaia, at this critical time … and be personally exempt?

Let it be very clear that i am not contemplating suicide. Suicide, for good reasons or bad, is the supreme act of saying 'no' to life – "I do not want this vale of tears". I say 'yes' to life, i love life and i don't want to go – any more than the warrior on the battlefield wants to go, any more than the 'community warrior' who dives into a stormy sea (say) trying to save a drowning person wants to go … any more than any of we values warriors, we 'yes-sayers' to life, will want to go, with so much still to do.

Woody Wood   May 2011

Revised by comments, criticisms and suggestions from friends and allies up to November 2014

BEFORE THE DELUGE

Some of them were dreamers
And some of them were fools
Who were making plans and thinking of the future
With the energy of the innocent
They were gathering the tools
They would need to make their journey back to nature
While the sands slipped through the opening
And their hands reached for the golden ring
With their hearts they turned to each other's hearts for refuge
In the troubled years that came before the deluge

Some of them were angry
At the way the earth was abused
By the men who learned to forge her beauty into power
And they struggled to protect her from them
Only to be confused
By the magnitude of her fury in the final hour
And when the sand was gone and the time arrived
In the naked dawn only a few survived
And in attempts to understand a thing so simple and so huge
Believed that they were meant to live ... after the deluge

Extract from lyrics by Jackson Browne: track from 'Late For The Sky' album, 1974

Reference Notes

1. Friedrich Nietzsche, 1844-1900: 'Daybreak: Thoughts on the Prejudices of Morality', section 327. Cambridge University Press, 1997 paperback ISBN 0521599636

2. Ludwig Wittgenstein 1889-1951: Compare the early 'Tractatus Logico-Philosophicus', Routledge Classics 2001 paperback edition. ISBN 0415254086 ... with the later 'Philosophical Investigations', Blackwell Publishing, 2001 paperback ISBN 0631231595

3. Term brought into modern use by Nietzsche in 'The Birth of Tragedy', O.U.P., 2008 paperback ISBN 0199540143 Dionysus: Greek god of wine, of revelry, ecstasy and immediacy, of the immeasurable.

4. Braziers: Braziers Park School of Integrative Social Research. BPSISR www.braziers.org Founded 1950

5. See note 3 above. Apollo: Greek god of many attributes, including form, reason, light and knowledge - yet capable (like science) of bringing plague as well as positive bounties.

6. Albert Einstein 1879-1955: Swiss scientist, renowned for the special and general theories of relativity. His famous formula: $E = mc^2$ told of the massive energy locked up in atoms ... leading to the atomic bomb and Hiroshima.

7. Henri and Henriette Frankfort, John A. Wilson, Thorkild Jacobsen: 'Before Philosophy', Penguin Books, 1971 paperback ISBN 014020198X Drawing on archaeological fieldwork in Egypt and Mesopotamia, explores the changing ways of knowing the world from the ancients to the Israelites to the Greeks. Quote is from the second page of the introductory chapter.

8. e.g. Richard Feynman: 'Cargo Cult Science' in Engineering and Science N° 37, June 1974, pp 10-13 "Integrity is the most important part of the scientific method, although it is not specifically included in any university course..."

9. F. Nietzsche: 'Beyond Good and Evil', Part 7, sect 225, Penguin Classics, 2003 paperback ISBN 014044923X

10. Arthur Schopenhauer, 1788-1860: 'The World as Will and Idea', Everyman, 1995 paperback ISBN 0460875051

11. F. Nietzsche: 'Thus Spoke Zarathustra', Penguin Classics, 1969 paperback ISBN 0140441182 Quote from The Second Dance Song, Part Three

12. Sigmund Freud 1856-1939: 'Collected Works', Bibliobazaar, 2008 hardcover ISBN 0554371243 The 'Father' of psychoanalysis abandoned the early idea that mental disorders were due to *brain* lesions in favour of engaging directly with the *minds* of his patients.

13. Behavioural Psychology. e.g. B. F. Skinner, 1904-1990: 'About Behaviourism', Knopf Publishing Group, 1988 paperback ISBN 0394716183 The dominant psychology of

the middle decades of the twentieth century. Famous for running mats through mazes.

14. Richard Dawkins: e.g. 'Unweaving The Rainbow', Penguin Group, 1998 hardback ISBN 071399241X One of many examples of his thought provoking contributions. In this book Dawkins attempts to hit back at his critics by arguing that seeing the grandeur and beauty of Nature is not incompatible with scientific rigour. Unfortunately the science of this hard line Neo-Darwinist is being bypassed by new broader understandings. Neither Fritjof Capra nor Rupert Sheldrake receive even a critical mention.   See also note 37.

15. Norman O. Brown, 1913-2002: 'Life Against Death: The Psychoanalytic Meaning of History', Wesleyan U.P., 1986 paperback ISBN 0819561444 Radical Neo-Freudian with an early deep critique of global capitalism.

16. Fritjof Capra: 'The Web of Life', Flamingo, 1997 paperback ISBN 0006547516 Application of Systems Theory to the active networks of pre-living and living structures. Pathfinding a new science. See also 'The Hidden Connections', Flamingo, 2010 paperback ISBN 0006551580 A further step towards a broader view of our world. Unfortunately, the transfer of his integrative systems approach to the social sphere is compromised by the present limitations of social psychology: no concepts of structure, complementary types, mode flips or group size effects.

17. Aristotle, 384-322 BCE: Eudemian Ethics, Oxford U.P., 2011 paperback ISBN 0199586438 Greek philosopher-scientist. Rejected his tutor Plato's idealist and state-centralist outlook for a more pluralist and pragmatic approach.

18. Ivan Illich, 1926-2002: 'Towards a History of Needs', Heyday Books, 1987 paperback ISBN 0930588266 This example describes some of the effects of going through the Second Threshold in social organisation. Generally, Illich opposed technocratic regulated society with a vision of a low tech, self-actuating, 'convivial' society. Introduced some important concepts.

19. Julian Jaynes, 1920-1997: 'The Origin of Consciousness in the Breakdown of the Bicameral Mind', Mariner Books, 2000 paperback edition ISBN 0618057072 Brings together a wealth of supporting evidence for this provocative thesis.

20. Lancelot Law Whyte, 1896-1972: 'The Next Development in Man', (first published Cresset Press 1944), Transaction Publications, 2002 paperback edition ISBN 0765809699

21. Karl Marx, 1818-1883: Quote from the introduction to his 'Critique of Hegel's Philosophy of Right', Cambridge U.P., 1977 paperback ISBN 0521292115 Several other revolutionary thinkers, including Bakunin, make this point about the social function of transcendental religion. The anarchist ditty has it: "Work and pray, live on hay, there'll be pie in the sky, by and by."

22. Isaac Asimov, 1920-1992: In 'Foundations Edge', Collins, 1994 paperback ISBN 0586058397, Galaxia is described as "A living organism which contains all the life forms and other non-living material in the Galaxy."

23. Nietzsche: 'Twilight of the Idols + The Antichrist', Cathedral Classics, 2010 paperback ISBN 1907523699

24. Robert Ardrey, 1908-1980: 'The Social Contract', Collins, 1970 hardback   ISBN 0002117908   Many of the chapters in this examination of social animals are major essays in their own right. The chapter 'Death by Stress' has relevance to the Ecology and Values Story.

25. Friedrich Engels, 1820-1895: 'The Origin of the Family, Private Property and the State', International Publishers, 1995 paperback ISBN 0717803597

26. Nicholas Georgescu-Roegen, 1906-1994: 'Energy and Economic Myths', Pergamon Press, 1976 paperback, ISBN 0080210279   An economics treatise drawing on the insights of thermodynamics, with some significant social implications.

27. Common Wealth began life as a small non-Fabian socialist party, founded in 1942 and winning some by-elections on its radical 'wealth in common' programme. Later a pressure group and think tank. Helped to develop a critique of the managerial society that was superseding the older owning class power. Supported syndicalism and English regionalism. Instrumental in the formation of both the Common Ownership Movement and Braziers Park S.I.S.R. Finally dissolved in 1993. Its written history (by J.C. Banks) has yet to be published.

28. Leopold Kohr, 1909-1994: 'The Breakdown of Nations', Green Books, 2001 paperback ISBN 1870098986 Also 'The Overdeveloped Nations', Schocken Books, 1978 hardback   ISBN 080523683X

29. E.F. Schumacher, 1911-1977: 'Small is Beautiful', Hartley & Marks, 2000 paperback ISBN 0881791695 Also 'A Guide for The Perplexed', Vintage Books, 2011 paperback ISBN 0099480212

30. Braziers Park S.I.S.R.: See note 4.

31. Wilfred Trotter, 1872-1939: 'Instincts of The Herd in Peace and War', Pranava Books, 2009 paperback   ISBN 1150070048 One of the primary influences on the early Braziers.

32. *Devolve!*: Founded 1988 as Movement For Middle England, a Midlands based devolution movement. Evolved into a small England-wide movement aiming at integration of, and support for, all aspects of devolution. Latterly a loose network and think tank trying also to relate the pluralist tradition to anticipated future events. www.devolve.org

33. Alfred Adler, 1870-1937: 'The Practice and Theory of Individual Psychology', Routledge, 1999 Hardcover ISBN 0415210518 Psychoanalytic pioneer. Broke with both Freud and Jung over their fixations with the id and the deep unconscious. Emphasis on the conscious ego, its modes and behaviour, its drive to power; ego interactions and 'games'. Transactional Analysis is one development of Adlerian thought.

34. Robert Ardrey: See note 24.

35. Morton Deutsch: 'The Resolution of Conflict: Constructive and Destructive Processes', Yale U.P., 1977 paperback   ISBN 0300021860   One of the few investigators to place human types/modes in a social context rather than merely a personal or psychoanalytical context.

36. Spiral Dynamics: System of social types mapping evolved from studies in the USA, with an added historical or time dimension. See note 46 for more reference.

37. Richard Dawkins: (Author of 'The Selfish Gene'; 'The Extended Phenotype') Here see the final chapter 'The Ballooning Mind' of 'Unweaving The Rainbow' (note 14) for reference to memes.

38. Susan Blackmore: 'The Meme Machine', Oxford Paperbacks, 2000 ISBN 019286212X Blackmore has introduced the concept 'Teme' as a third replicator hosted by machines much as memes are hosted by our minds and genes by our bodies.

39. Ian Brown: private communication. One of many contributions critical to the development of this essay.

40. Karl Marx: 'Das Kapital', Regnery Publishing Inc., 2009 paperback ISBN 08952 6711X

41. Thorstein Veblen, 1857-1929: 'The Theory of the Leisure Class', Oxford U.P., 2009 paperback ISBN 0199552584 An economics thesis (in 1899) relatively ignored by economists until recently, yet widely influential in sociology.

42. F. Nietzsche: 'Beyond Good and Evil', Part 9, sect 257. See note 9.

43. John Fletcher: 'The Secret People', Essay published in 'Undercurrents', issue 19, 1976/7 Reprints available from *Devolve!* inform@devolve.org

44. F. Nietzsche: 'Thus Spoke Zarathustra', Part one, "of the 1001 goals" Wordsworth Editions, 1997 paperback ISBN 1853267767

45. B. A. Wood: '1971 Essay' (no formal title or publication) Serialised in 1974/5 in 'Undercurrents' magazine, issues 10 to 13. Extract published in 'International Associations' (bi-lingual), February 1975 issue. Copies from *Devolve!* on request.

46. Clare W Graves, 1914-1986: Pioneer of what became the Spiral Dynamics model of social types. See for example 'The Never Ending Quest: A Treatise on an Emergent Cyclical Conception of Adult Behavioural Systems and their Development', Eclet Publishing, 2005 hardback ISBN 0972474218   See also note 34.

47. Postmodernism: For an introduction to this complex subject see 'Introducing Post-Modernism', Appignanesi and Garratt, Icon Books, 2007 paperback edition. ISBN 1840468491

48. Norman O. Brown: 'Life Against Death: The Psychoanalytic Meaning of History'. See note 15.

49. John Gray: 'Enlightenment's Wake', Routledge, 1995 hardback edition ISBN 0415124751 A collection of essays that does what it says in the title.

50. Charles Darwin, 1809-1892: 'On the Origin of Species', Dover Publications Inc...., 2006 paperback ISBN 0486450066 Darwin's less dogmatic stance has been justified in the light of the developing science of Epigenetics, which demonstrates quasi-Lamarckian effects and incidentally vindicates some of Sheldrake's arguments of earlier decades.

51. Rupert Sheldrake: 'A New Science Of Life' Icon Books, 2009 paperback edition ISBN 978 1848310421 Despite the compelling argument critics object that it is not compatible with Apollonian science, the science of the outside of the Universe. Exactly. This also applies to his 'Dogs That Know When Their Owners Are Coming Home', Crown Publishing, 2000 paperback edition 0609805339

52. Richard Leakey and Roger Lewin: 'The Sixth Extinction', Weidenfeld and Nicolson, 1996 paperback edition ISBN 0297817477 Taken as a whole, provides the long view

and the broad picture of the present extinction process. The backdrop to the Ecology and Values story.

53. Lynne Margulis and Dorian Sagan: 'Acquiring Genomes', Basic Books, 2003 paperback ISBN 0465043925 A further challenge to Neo-Darwinist orthodoxy.

54. Robert Ardrey: 'The Social Contract'. See note 24.

55. Herbert Spencer, 1820-1903: 'First Principles', Adamant Media Corp., 2000 paperback ISBN 1402199791 The originator of Social Darwinism. Very influential in his time.

56. Ferdinand Tönnies: 'Gemeinschaft und Gessellschaft' (Community and Society), Dover Publications, 2011 paperback, ISBN 0486424979 See also 'The Alienation of Modern Man' by Fritz Pappenheim, Monthly Review Press, 2010 paperback ISBN 0853450056

57. Network Project: A radical think tank, active 2000 to 2008.

58. Sigmund Freud. See note 12.

59. Victor Serge, 1890-1947: Anarchist revolutionary, writer and poet. 'Memoirs of A Revolutionary', NYRB Classics, 2012 paperback ISBN 1590174518

60. For one text locating The Chakra in Eastern philosophy and practice: 'An Introduction to Hinduism', Gavin Flood, Cambridge University Press, 1996 paperback ISBN 0521438780

61. Konrad Lorenz, 1903-1989: 'On Aggression', Routledge, 2002 Paperback ISBN 0415283205 Pioneering, influential and controversial ethologist.

62. Herbert Marcuse, 1898-1979: 'One Dimensional Man', Routledge, 2002 paperback ISBN 0415289777 also 'Eros and Civilization', Sphere Books, 1956 Hardback (out of print new) ISBN 978 0415186636

63. Norman O. Brown. See notes 15 and 48.

64. John Hewetson: 'Sexual Freedom for The Young', Freedom Press, 1951 Card Covers, no known ISBN. Reprinted 1987 as article in The Raven N° 4 (see below)

65. Colin Ward, 1924-2010: Anarchist architect, writer, historian. His preface to above article records concern over population with regard to appropriate housing.

66. The Raven: Anarchist quarterly journal published until 2003. Used copies of some issues still available.

67. Wilhelm Reich, 1897-1957: 'The Sexual Revolution', Farrar-Strauss-Giroux, 1986 paperback ISBN 0374502692 'The Function of The Orgasm', Souvenir Press, 1989 paperback ISBN 0285649701

68. Bronislaw Malinowski, 1884-1942: 'The Sexual Life of Savages in North West Melanesia', Kessinger Publications, 2010 paperback ISBN 1162769517

69. Maureen Boustred, former educator; Park Homes campaigner and *Devolve!* network member:

70. 'Towards Human Ecology' published as article in The Raven N° 15 (see above)

71. Elwin Verrier, 1902-1964: 'The Muria and Their Ghotul', OUP (Delhi), 1991 paperback ISBN 0195628535

72. The Woodcraft Folk. Youth movement. Like The Order of Woodcraft Chivalry (which still has links with Braziers Park) evolved in 1920's-30's as a more radical and

co-operative alternative to the Scout movement. Allied movements in over sixty countries. www.woodcraft.org.uk

73. Ferdinand Mount: see note 76 below.

74. Wilfred Trotter: see note 31.

75. Bruce Bagemihl: 'Biological Exuberance: Homosexuality and Natural Diversity', St Martins Press, 2005 paperback ISBN 031225377X

76. Ferdinand Mount: 'Mind The Gap', Short Books, 2005 paperback ISBN 1904977324 Courageous re-appraisal by a Conservative thinker in the radical Disraeli tradition of the value and dignity of the working class culture that emerged from the industrial revolution – essentially a pluralist civil society – and its subsequent dis-empowerment by the threatened middle classes and the Fabian-Jacobin State ... leading eventually to the Downers (his term) of today: an underclass without structure or hope.

77. William Morris, 1834-1896: Creative artist and visionary thinker whose journey from comfortable liberal to revolutionary socialist certainly made him 'a traitor to his class'. e.g. 'News From Nowhere', Oxford U.P., 2009 paperback ISBN 0199539197

78. Richard Leakey and Roger Lewin: see note 52.

79. Adam Smith, 1723-1790: compare 'The Wealth of Nations', Harriman House Publishing, 2007 hardback ISBN 1905641265 ... with 'The Theory of Moral Sentiments', Penguin, 2010 paperback ISBN 0143105922

80. Transition Network: aiming, through localism, to prepare communities for life beyond oil: www.transitionnetwork.org

81. Population Matters: formerly Optimum Population Trust; founded as a voice in the silence on the population question after an unholy alliance of the liberal Left and the religious Right made it an un-mentionable issue for decades. That censorship is at last crumbling and Population Matters may take at least some of the credit. www.populationmatters.org

82. James Lovelock: Independent scientist, originator, with Lynne Margulis, of the Gaia Hypothesis. In recent books increasingly concerned over what we humans are doing to the planet. e.g. 'The Revenge of Gaia', Penguin, 2007 paperback ISBN 0141025972

83. Frederick M. Thrasher: 'The Gang: A Study of 1,313 Gangs in Chicago', Routledge, 2005 hardcover ISBN 0415700965

84. Mirror Neurones: see for example 'Social Intelligence: the New Science of Human Relationships', Daniel Goleman, Hutchinson, 2006 hardback ISBN 978 0091799434

85. Revaluation Co-counselling: "... a process whereby people of all ages and backgrounds can exchange effective help to free themselves from the effects of past hurts." www.rc.org

86. William Cobbett (1763 – 1835) in early life may be considered an anti-Jacobin Tory but was increasingly radicalised by the corruption of the political system and the deteriorating condition of the rural poor. His 'Political Register' was published for over thirty years and was the most widely read working class paper – feared by the establishment. A prolific writer on many subjects, his most widely known work is 'Rural Rides in The Counties', reissued by Cambridge University Press, 2009 paperback ISBN 0140435794

87. George Orwell: 'The Lion and The Unicorn', Penguin, 1990 paperback ISBN 0140182373

88. Albert Camus, 'The Rebel'. Quoted in Stan Rowe: 'Earth Alive: Essays on Ecology', NeWest Press, 2006 paperback ISBN 9781897126035 p238.

89. Lovelock and Leakey: See notes 78 and 52.

90. John Gray: 'Straw Dogs', Granta Books, 2002 paperback edition ISBN 1862075692 His later works increasingly pessimistic.

91. Club of Rome: Actually a report to the Club of Rome by a team from the Massachusetts Institute of Technology (M.I.T.). Based on computer simulations of population, per capita income and production trends with various different assumptions about available resources, pollution, and other factors. Pan Books, 1975 paperback ISBN 0330241699 As scary as the report itself were the reactions of denial of its message.

92. Spiral Dynamics: see notes 36 and 46.

93. Herbert Spencer: see note 54.

94. Konrad Kwiet and Jurgen Matthaus: 'Contemporary Responses to The Holocaust', Greenwood Press, 2004 hardcover ISBN 0275974669

95. The extreme secrecy of the Israeli State, especially in the field of weapons research, makes the verification of such claims difficult. This is compounded by the undoubted bias of some sources. For two assessments of the weapons research programme from credible non-radical sources: 'Gideon's Spies: The Secret History of The Mossad' by Gordon Thomas, St Martin's Press, 1999 paperback ISBN 0312252846 and 'Proliferation of Weapons of Mass Destruction: Assessing the Risks', US Congress Office of Technology Assessment, 1993 OTA-ISC-559 (Retrieved 2008)

96. Club of Rome: see note 91.

97. Weird: although translated here as fate, Weird in the Northern Pagan tradition was a much bigger concept, almost a universal force, inspiring both humility and stoicism as a human response. Even the gods were subject to Weird. The modern trivial meaning reflects the suppression of that tradition.

SOME OTHER SOURCES OF INSIGHT

Just four from many that could be included:

A. 'Population vs. Liberty', Jack Parsons, Pemberton Books, 1971 hardback SBN 301710511   The Population Issue confronted in terms of human wellbeing.

B. 'The Social Philosophers', Robert Nisbet, Paladin/Granada Publishing, 1976 paperback SBN 586082158   The social history of forms of responses to the need for community.

C. 'Chaos', James Gleick, Penguin Books, 1988 paperback   ISBN 0140092501   Chronicles a challenge from nature to the certainties and arrogance of the old science.

D. 'The Pluralist Theory of The State – selected writings', Routledge, 1993 paperback   ISBN 0415033713   Edited with an extended and wise introduction by Paul Q. Hirst. Charts the thinking, the struggles and the defeat of early twentieth century Pluralism before both increasing centralism of the Jacobin-Fabian State and the meme of statism among crucial sections of the Labour movement.

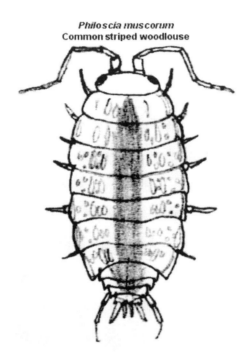

Philoscia muscorum
Common striped woodlouse